# Stretch Your Thinking

## ENRICHMENT WORKBOOK

**Harcourt Brace & Company**

Orlando • Atlanta • Austin • Boston • San Francisco • Chicago • Dallas • New York • Toronto • London

*http://www.hbschool.com*

Printed in the United States of America

ISBN 0-15-311081-3

6 7 8 9 10 085 2000

# CONTENTS

# Balance the Scales

Write the number that is missing on one side of the scale. The sum of each pair of numbers should be the same. Write the sum in the scale's base. The first one is completed for you.

1.  _4_ + _6_        _3_ + _7_
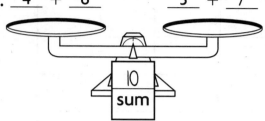

2.  _2_ + _8_        ___ + _9_

3.  _9_ + _1_        _5_ + ___
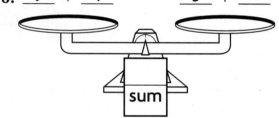

4.  _8_ + _4_        _10_ + ___
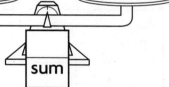

5.  _9_ + _6_        _10_ + ___
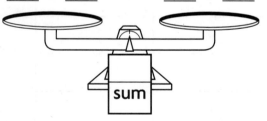

6.  _7_ + _5_        _11_ + ___
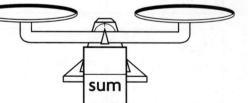

7.  _9_ + ___        _10_ + _7_
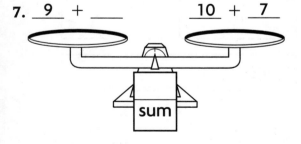

8.  _8_ + ___        _10_ + _5_

9.  _9_ + _3_        _10_ + ___
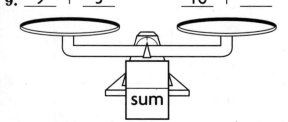

10. _8_ + ___        _10_ + _1_
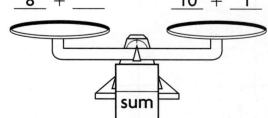

# What Is My Rule?

Guess each rule. Then write the missing numbers.

1.

| Rule: add 2 | |
|---|---|
| 4 | 6 |
| 7 | 9 |
| 3 | 5 |
| 9 | 11 |
| 6 | 8 |
| 34 | 36 |

2.

| Rule: add 9 | |
|---|---|
| 2 | 11 |
| 5 | 14 |
| 6 | 15 |
| 8 | 17 |
| 4 | 13 |
| 7 | 16 |

3.

| Rule: subtract 2 | |
|---|---|
| 9 | 7 |
| 6 | 4 |
| 3 | 1 |
| 5 | 3 |
| 8 | 6 |
| 2 | 0 |

4.

| Rule: Doubles | |
|---|---|
| 4 | 8 |
| 3 | 6 |
| 9 | 18 |
| 5 | 10 |
| 6 | 12 |
| 10 | 20 |

5.

| Rule: Make 10 | |
|---|---|
| 4 | 6 |
| 2 | 8 |
| 1 | 9 |
| 5 | 5 |
| 3 | 7 |

6.

| Rule: add + 10 | |
|---|---|
| 3 | 13 |
| 7 | 17 |
| 5 | 15 |
| 8 | 18 |
| 4 | 14 |

# Addition Squares

Follow these steps to find the sum of
the four numbers.

- Add the two numbers in each row.

- Add the two numbers in each column.

- Add the two numbers in the last row,
  and add the two numbers in the last
  column. The sums should be the same.
  Write the sum in the circle.

| 1 | 2 | 3 |
|---|---|---|
| 3 | 4 | 7 |
| 4 | 6 | (10) |

---

Write the missing numbers.

**1.**

| 5 | 4 | |
|---|---|---|
| 2 | 6 | |
| | | ◯ |

**2.**

| 2 | 6 | |
|---|---|---|
| 6 | 2 | |
| | | ◯ |

**3.**

| 0 | 5 | |
|---|---|---|
| 4 | 3 | |
| | | ◯ |

**4.**

| 0 | 4 | |
|---|---|---|
| 7 | 0 | |
| | | ◯ |

**5.**

| 4 | 4 | |
|---|---|---|
| 3 | 3 | |
| | | ◯ |

**6.**

| 7 | 2 | |
|---|---|---|
| 1 | 3 | |
| | | ◯ |

**7.**

| | 3 | 7 |
|---|---|---|
| 2 | | |
| | 6 | ◯ |

**8.**

| 4 | | 9 |
|---|---|---|
| | | 6 |
| 7 | | ◯ |

**9.**

| | | |
|---|---|---|
| 3 | 0 | |
| 3 | 5 | ◯ |

# Bump-It Addition

## Directions

- Work with a partner.

- Trace and cut out the number pieces and put them in a bag.

- Take turns choosing two number pieces. Add the numbers and place a marker on the sum on the gameboard. If a square has your partner's marker on it, you may bump off the marker.

- When all the number pieces have been used, put them back in the bag and continue to play.

- The winner is the first player to get four markers in a row.

**Number Pieces**

| 1 | 2 | 3 | 4 | 5 | 6 | 7 | 8 | 9 |
|---|---|---|---|---|---|---|---|---|
| 1 | 2 | 3 | 4 | 5 | 6 | 7 | 8 | 9 |

**Gameboard**

| 5  | 6  | 14 | 17 | 4  |
|----|----|----|----|----|
| 10 | 18 | 2  | 11 | 9  |
| 16 | 3  | 9  | 15 | 11 |
| 8  | 8  | 6  | 13 | 12 |
| 12 | 7  | 13 | 10 | 7  |

# Riddle, Riddle

## Why do birds fly south in the winter?

Write the answer for each subtraction problem. Then use the code to write the matching letter below each answer. Read across to answer the riddle.

**Code**

| 0 | 1 | 2 | 3 | 4 | 5 | 6 | 7 | 8 | 9 |
|---|---|---|---|---|---|---|---|---|---|
| A | F | I | K | L | O | R | S | T | W |

1.  $\begin{array}{r} 11 \\ -9 \\ \hline \square \end{array}$  2.  $\begin{array}{r} 17 \\ -9 \\ \hline \square \end{array}$   3.  $\begin{array}{r} 10 \\ -8 \\ \hline \square \end{array}$  4.  $\begin{array}{r} 16 \\ -9 \\ \hline \square \end{array}$

_____   _____          _____   _____

5.  $\begin{array}{r} 16 \\ -8 \\ \hline \square \end{array}$  6.  $\begin{array}{r} 13 \\ -8 \\ \hline \square \end{array}$  7.  $\begin{array}{r} 14 \\ -9 \\ \hline \square \end{array}$    8.  $\begin{array}{r} 10 \\ -9 \\ \hline \square \end{array}$  9.  $\begin{array}{r} 9 \\ -9 \\ \hline \square \end{array}$  10.  $\begin{array}{r} 15 \\ -9 \\ \hline \square \end{array}$

_____   _____   _____          _____   _____   _____

11.  $\begin{array}{r} 14 \\ -6 \\ \hline \square \end{array}$  12.  $\begin{array}{r} 11 \\ -6 \\ \hline \square \end{array}$    13.  $\begin{array}{r} 18 \\ -9 \\ \hline \square \end{array}$  14.  $\begin{array}{r} 8 \\ -8 \\ \hline \square \end{array}$  15.  $\begin{array}{r} 13 \\ -9 \\ \hline \square \end{array}$  16.  $\begin{array}{r} 12 \\ -9 \\ \hline \square \end{array}$

_____   _____          _____   _____   _____   _____!

**17.** Write your own riddle.

_____

_____

_____

# Letter Logic

Fill in the answers.

A and B stand for numbers.

1. If A is 3, then B is _____.

2. If A is 9, then B is _____.

3. If B is 1, then A is _____.

4. If B is 7, then A is _____.

5. 9 − B is _____.

6. 9 − A is _____.

$$\begin{array}{r} A \\ +\ B \\ \hline 9 \end{array}$$

C and D stand for numbers.

7. If C is 8, then D is _____.

8. If C is 2, then D is _____.

9. If D is 5, then C is _____.

10. If D is 1, then C is _____.

$$\begin{array}{r} C \\ -\ 2 \\ \hline D \end{array}$$

X, Y, and Z stand for numbers.

11. If X is 4 and Y is 2, then Z is _____.

12. If X is 9 and Y is 4, then Z is _____.

13. If X is 5 and Z is 8, then Y is _____.

14. If X is 9 and Z is 12, then Y is _____.

15. Name two numbers that X and Y might be if Z is 15.

_____

# Equal Sums

Fill in the missing digits so that the sum of the 3 digits in
each straight line is the same.

**1.**

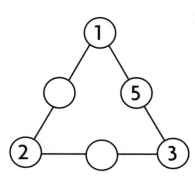

sum = _____

**2.**

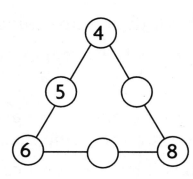

sum = _____

**3.**

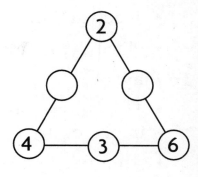

sum = _____

**4.**

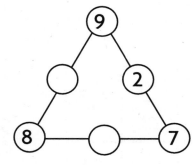

sum = _____

**5.**

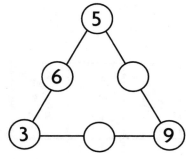

sum = _____

**6.**

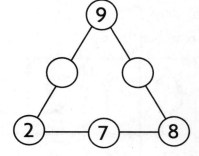

sum = _____

**7.**

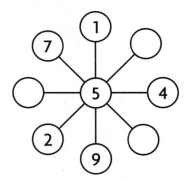

sum = _____

**8.**

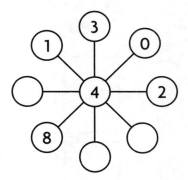

sum = _____

# The Greater Sum Wins!

Play with a partner.

**Getting Ready to Play:**

- Trace and then cut out the number pieces.

- Place the number pieces into a paper bag.

**To Play:**

- Take turns choosing a number piece and placing it in one of the 4 spaces on the game board.

- After each player has filled a game board, find and record the sum.

- Check each other's sum.

- Put the number pieces back and play again.

**Number Pieces**

| 0 | 1 | 2 | 3 | 4 | 5 | 6 | 7 | 8 | 9 |
|---|---|---|---|---|---|---|---|---|---|
| 0 | 1 | 2 | 3 | 4 | 5 | 6 | 7 | 8 | 9 |

**Game Board
Player 1**

**Game Board
Player 2**

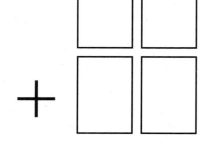

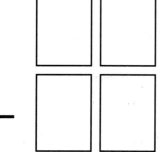

# Break the Code

In the addition problems below, each letter stands for a digit. The same letter stands for the same digit in all of the problems.

The table shows that G = 1. Use the addition problems to find out what each of the other letters stands for. Once you have broken the code, you can answer the riddle at the bottom of the page.

| 0 | 1 | 2 | 3 | 4 | 5 | 6 | 7 | 8 | 9 |
|---|---|---|---|---|---|---|---|---|---|
|   | G |   |   |   |   |   |   |   |   |

**1.**
```
  G G        11
+G G       +11
-----      ----
  A A
```

**2.**
```
  A G
+A A
-----
  I B
```

**3.**
```
  G B
+A I
-----
  B N
```

**4.**
```
  A N
+G B
-----
  I S
```

**5.**
```
  I N
+I N
-----
  P I
```

**6.**
```
  G P
+A P
-----
  I E
```

**7.**
```
  B P
+B Y
-----
  N I
```

**8.**
```
  E G
+E G
-----
G L A
```

Can anything be smarter than a cat that can count?

| Code Letter | | | | | | | | | | | | | | | | |
|---|---|---|---|---|---|---|---|---|---|---|---|---|---|---|---|---|
| Digit | 5 | 8 | 0 | 2 | 0 | 9 | 8 | 6 | 6 | 4 | 7 | 1 | 3 | 8 | 8 | ! |

# Nature's Numbers

1. Mr. Jackson bought a globe and a bird feeder. About how much money did he spend?

_____

2. Mrs. Wilson bought a whale shirt, a stuffed penguin, and a bear book. About how much money did she spend?

_____

3. Ms. Hill spent about $60. She bought a bear book and a

_____.

4. Mr. Curtis spent about $90. He bought a microscope and a

_____.

5. Ms. Hunter spent $100. She bought a whale shirt, binoculars, and a

_____.

6. Mr. Morgan spent about $70. He bought binoculars and a

_____.

7. You can spend about $80 at the gift shop. You want to buy 3 gifts that are the same or different. You could buy

_____, _____, and _____ or

_____, _____, and _____.

# Tag It

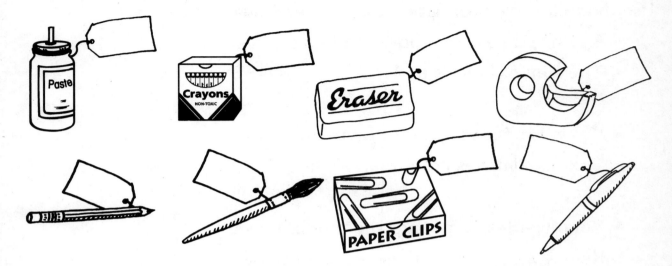

1. Use the clues to find the price of each item. Write the price on each price tag.

   • Eric had 50¢. After he bought a pencil, he had 40¢ left.

   • Pat bought a pencil and an eraser. He spent 35¢.

   • The pen costs 49¢ more than the pencil.

   • Laura bought a pencil and a box of paper clips. She spent 75¢.

   • Meg paid 75¢ for tape. Her change was 1¢.

   • A jar of paste costs the same amount as 8 pencils.

   • Zachary bought 2 pencils and a paint brush. He spent 61¢.

   • A box of crayons costs 33¢ more than a pen.

2. Jessica bought an eraser and a box of paper clips. How much money did she spend?

   _____

3. Anna has 80¢. How much more money does she need to buy a box of crayons?

   _____

4. Which costs more: 3 erasers or a jar of paste?

   _____

5. Which costs less: 4 pencils or a paint brush?

   _____

# Measure Up

Use the following information to complete the chart below.

- Kevin is 2 years younger than Luisa.
- The sum of Luisa's and Yoko's ages is 18.

- Kevin is 5 inches shorter than Luisa.
- Yoko is 9 inches taller than Kevin.

- Yoko weighs 12 pounds more than Luisa.
- Kevin weighs 11 pounds less than Luisa.

- Yoko has twice as many pets as Luisa.
- Luisa, Kevin, and Yoko have 12 pets in all.

- There are twice as many pets as people in Kevin's family.
- There are the same number of people and pets in Yoko's family.
- Luisa's family has 2 more people than Kevin's family.

| | Kevin | Luisa | Yoko |
|---|---|---|---|
| Age | 6 | | |
| Height (in inches) | | 50 | |
| Weight (in pounds) | | | 69 |
| Number of Pets | | 2 | |
| Number of Family Members | | | |

# Subtract to Win

Work with a partner.

**Materials:**

• Base-ten blocks, including 20 tens, 40 ones

• Two number cubes, with numbers 1–6

**How to Play:**

The object of the game is to get rid of all of your blocks by paying them to the bank.

Each player starts with 10 tens.

Select a banker for each game. That person collects and trades the blocks and also plays.

Take turns. Roll the number cubes and add the numbers shown. Pay the bank the number of ones blocks equal to the sum. If you do not have enough ones blocks, trade a ten for 10 ones at the bank.

| Tens | Ones |
|------|------|
|      |      |
|      |      |
|      |      |
|      |      |
|      |      |

# Subtract and Search

Answer each of the 13 subtraction exercises below.

Shade in each answer on the number chart.

| 1 | 2 | 3 | 4 | 5 | 6 | 7 | 8 | 9 | 10 |
|---|---|---|---|---|---|---|---|---|---|
| 11 | 12 | 13 | 14 | 15 | 16 | 17 | 18 | 19 | 20 |
| 21 | 22 | 23 | 24 | 25 | 26 | 27 | 28 | 29 | 30 |
| 31 | 32 | 33 | 34 | 35 | 36 | 37 | 38 | 39 | 40 |
| 41 | 42 | 43 | 44 | 45 | 46 | 47 | 48 | 49 | 50 |

1.  $\begin{array}{r} 61 \\ -58 \\ \hline \end{array}$

2.  $\begin{array}{r} 71 \\ -28 \\ \hline \end{array}$

3.  $\begin{array}{r} 43 \\ -16 \\ \hline \end{array}$

4.  $\begin{array}{r} 43 \\ -18 \\ \hline \end{array}$

5.  $\begin{array}{r} 92 \\ -45 \\ \hline \end{array}$

6.  $\begin{array}{r} 52 \\ -29 \\ \hline \end{array}$

7.  $\begin{array}{r} 48 \\ -35 \\ \hline \end{array}$

8.  $\begin{array}{r} 84 \\ -67 \\ \hline \end{array}$

9.  $\begin{array}{r} 89 \\ -75 \\ \hline \end{array}$

10.  $\begin{array}{r} 62 \\ -29 \\ \hline \end{array}$

11.  $\begin{array}{r} 55 \\ -48 \\ \hline \end{array}$

12.  $\begin{array}{r} 98 \\ -61 \\ \hline \end{array}$

13.  $\begin{array}{r} 94 \\ -78 \\ \hline \end{array}$

14. What letter is shaded in the number chart? _____

15. What position is this letter in the alphabet?

_____

# Choose the Matching Problem

Fill in the missing numbers in each subtraction exercise.
Draw a line from the subtraction exercise to the related
addition exercise.

**1.**　8　0
－☐☐
————
　　　6

**A.**　☐☐
＋ 1　5
————
　4　0

**2.**　9　0
－☐☐
————
　6　4

**B.**　2　2
＋☐☐
————
　7　0

**3.**　7　0
－☐☐
————
　3　1

**C.**　☐☐
＋ 6　4
————
　9　0

**4.**　4　0
－☐☐
————
　1　5

**D.**　1　3
＋☐☐
————
　3　0

**5.**　7　0
－☐☐
————
　2　2

**E.**　☐☐
＋　　6
————
　8　0

**6.**　3　0
－☐☐
————
　1　3

**F.**　3　1
＋☐☐
————
　7　0

# Yard Sale Bargains

Liz is selling some of her toys at a yard sale.

1. Rob buys the book. He gives Liz 75¢. What is his change?

_____

2. Cora spends exactly 80¢. What 2 items does she buy?

_____

3. Steve buys the jump rope and the car. What is his change from 90¢?

_____

4. Angela buys the puppet. She gives Liz 50¢. What is her change?

_____

5. How much more does the jump rope cost than the car?

_____

6. David wants to buy the boat, but he has only 55¢. How much money does he need to borrow?

_____

7. Tom buys the pinwheel. He gives Liz 1 dime and 2 nickels. What is his change?

_____

8. Liz begins working at the yard sale at 8:00 A.M. She sells the last toy at 11:30 A.M. How much time does she spend at the yard sale?

_____

# Family Measurements

The Bell family made a chart to show the age, height, and weight of each family member.

| Name | Age | Height (in inches) | Weight (in pounds) |
|------|-----|--------------------|--------------------|
| Grace | 5 | 42 | 39 |
| Ben | 8 | 50 | 57 |
| Theo | 12 | 58 | 83 |
| Mrs. Bell | 37 | 66 | 124 |
| Mr. Bell | 41 | 70 | 172 |

1. How much more does Ben weigh than Grace?

   _____

2. How much taller is Mr. Bell than Theo?

   _____

3. Ben and Theo sit together on one side of a seesaw. How much do they weigh in all?

   _____

4. Ben and Mrs. Bell have the same birthday. How old was Mrs. Bell when Ben was born?

   _____

5. Grace knows that 1 yard = 36 inches. How much taller than 1 yard is Grace?

   _____

6. Which two people have heights that add up to exactly 100 inches?

   _____

7. Each year on his birthday, Ben has a cake with the same number of candles as his age. How many birthday candles has Ben had on all of his cakes?

   _____

8. Ben said that the weights of all the children are more than the weight of Mr. Bell. Was he right?

   _____

Name _____

# Work Backward

Work backward to find the number that belongs in each
circle. Then look at the numbers beneath the blanks in the
puzzle below. Find the number that matches a number in a
circle. Write the letter that is next to the circle on the
blank above the number.

1. P ◯ → +2 → 39 → −3 → 36 → +10 → 46

2. D ◯ → −5 → 61 → −10 → 51 → +2 → 53

3. H ◯ → +5 → 78 → +20 → 98 → −8 → 90

4. S ◯ → +8 → 89 → −4 → 85 → −10 → 75

5. I ◯ → −7 → 52 → −30 → 22 → +7 → 29

6. R ◯ → +4 → 50 → −2 → 48 → −20 → 28

7. E ◯ → −10 → 82 → +6 → 88 → −9 → 79

8. A ◯ → −6 → 9 → +20 → 29 → +5 → 34

Why did the fly fly?

$\overline{15}$     $\overline{81}$   $\overline{37}$   $\overline{59}$   $\overline{66}$   $\overline{92}$   $\overline{46}$

$\overline{81}$   $\overline{37}$   $\overline{59}$   $\overline{92}$   $\overline{66}$     $\overline{73}$   $\overline{92}$   $\overline{46}$

# Palindromes

A *palindrome* is a word or phrase that reads the same forward and backward. Some examples are *Otto*, *Ada*, and *Madam, I'm Adam*.

Numbers can also be palindromes. Some examples are 88, 151, and 34,143. You can make your own number palindromes using addition. Look at the boxes.

Choose any 2- or 3-digit number. Reverse the digits.

$$\begin{array}{r} 14 \\ +41 \\ \hline \end{array}$$

Add. $\quad 55$

55 is a palindrome. It reads the same forward and backward.

Choose any 2- or 3-digit number.
Reverse the digits. $\quad 48$

$$\begin{array}{r} +84 \\ \hline \end{array}$$

Add. $\quad 132$

Reverse the digits $\quad 132$
of the sum. $\quad +231$

Add. $\quad \overline{363}$

The number 363 is a palindrome.

---

## Reverse and add until you get a palindrome.

| 1.    57 | 2.    153 | 3.    29 | 4.    261 |
|---|---|---|---|
| | | | |

Try this out with your own 2- or 3-digit numbers. For some numbers, you need to reverse and add many times before you get a palindrome. You may need an extra piece of paper.

| 5. | 6. | 7. | 8. |
|---|---|---|---|
| | | | |

# Adding Up

Play with a partner.

**Materials:** Two number cubes, paper, and pencil

**How to Play:**

- Players take turns. Roll the number cubes and form a 2-digit number. *Either digit may be in either place.* It is the player's decision.

- On your second turn, add the number rolled to the number you rolled on your first turn. After that, keep adding to form a larger sum on each turn.

- The game ends when one player reaches a sum of 400 or more.

**How to Score:**

- Score **5 points** whenever you reach a sum that ends in 5, such as 125.

- Score **10 points** whenever you reach a sum that ends in 0, such as 140 or 340.

- Score **50 points** if you are the first player to reach a sum of 400 or more.

- The player with the most points at the end of the game wins!

**Example:**

Turn 1:    42

Turn 2:    +52
                              94

Turn 3:    +36
                              130 → Score 10 points

Turn 4:    + 65
                              195 → Score 5 points

On Turn 3, the player could also form the number 63. The player would get a larger sum, but there would not be a score of 10 for that turn.

# Riddle Ride

Find each difference. Then look at the rows of boxes at the bottom of the page. Find the two numbers that the difference falls between. In the box between those two numbers, write the letter that is next to the difference.

**Example:**
```
   566
 − 199
   367   G
```

| | | | |
|---|---|---|---|
| 1.  956<br>− 280<br><br>　　　　　T | 2.  424<br>− 218<br><br>　　　　　Y | 3.  613<br>− 272<br><br>　　　　　N | 4.  435<br>− 390<br><br>　　　　　A |
| 5.  613<br>− 438<br><br>　　　　　L | 6.  756<br>− 255<br><br>　　　　　R | 7.  930<br>− 291<br><br>　　　　　E | 8.  425<br>− 126<br><br>　　　　　I |
| 9.  425<br>−  68<br><br>　　　　　G | 10.  920<br>− 360<br><br>　　　　　P | 11.  720<br>− 285<br><br>　　　　　C | 12.  456<br>− 344<br><br>　　　　　F |

## What kind of pet can you take a ride on?

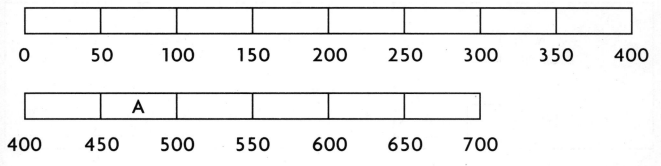

| 0 | 50 | 100 | 150 | 200 | 250 | 300 | 350 | 400 |
|---|---|---|---|---|---|---|---|---|

|   | A |   |   |   |   |
|---|---|---|---|---|---|

| 400 | 450 | 500 | 550 | 600 | 650 | 700 |
|---|---|---|---|---|---|---|

# Get in Shape

For each pair of number sentences, each shape represents a single number. You may use the strategy *guess and check* to figure out the number that each shape represents. Write the number inside the shape.

**Example:**

$7 + \boxed{5} = 12$

$7 - \boxed{5} = 2$

**1.**

$\bigcirc + \triangle = 15$

$\bigcirc - \triangle = 3$

**2.**

$\bigcirc + \square = 20$

$\bigcirc - \square = 10$

**3.**

$\bigcirc + \square = 100$

$\bigcirc - \square = 60$

**4.**

$\bigcirc + \triangle = 13$

$\bigcirc - \triangle = 5$

**5.**

$\triangle + \square = 7$

$\triangle - 1 = \square$

**6.**

$\bigcirc + \triangle = 16$

$\bigcirc - 2 = \triangle$

For Problems 7–8, there is more than one possible solution.

**7.**

$\triangle + \square = 10$

$10 - \square = \triangle$

**8.**

$8 - \triangle = \bigcirc$

$8 - \bigcirc = \triangle$

# Missing Digits

Fill in the missing digits.

1.
```
    3  0  ☐
  − 1  2  5
  ─────────
    1  ☐  5
```

2.
```
    5  0  0
  − 3  2  ☐
  ─────────
    ☐  7  3
```

3.
```
    ☐  0  0
  − 6  ☐  4
  ─────────
    2  6  6
```

4.
```
    5  0  ☐
  − 1  9  8
  ─────────
    3  ☐  5
```

5.
```
    6  ☐  1
  − 2  8  4
  ─────────
    3  1  ☐
```

6.
```
    7  0  7
  − 1  ☐  9
  ─────────
    5  5  ☐
```

7.
```
    4  0  ☐
  − 1  9  5
  ─────────
    ☐  0  5
```

8.
```
    ☐  0  0
  − 3  3  ☐
  ─────────
    3  6  8
```

9.
```
    ☐  0  4
  −    3  ☐
  ─────────
    6  5
```

Find the difference. Then check by adding.

10.
```
    5  0  0          1  2  5
  − 1  2  5        + ☐ ☐ ☐
  ─────────        ─────────
    ☐ ☐ ☐            5  0  0
```

11.
```
    7  0  0          3  5  9
  − 3  5  9        + ☐ ☐ ☐
  ─────────        ─────────
    ☐ ☐ ☐            7  0  0
```

12.
```
    4  0  7          1  2  9
  − 1  2  9        + ☐ ☐ ☐
  ─────────        ─────────
    ☐ ☐ ☐            4  0  7
```

13.
```
    9  0  2          ☐ ☐ ☐
  − 1  3  5        + 1  3  5
  ─────────        ─────────
    ☐ ☐ ☐            9  0  2
```

# Snack Bar Subtraction

| Snack Bar Menu | | | |
|---|---|---|---|
| Hamburger | $2.25 | Apple | $0.55 |
| Grilled Cheese | $1.50 | Orange | $0.45 |
| Hot Dog | $1.30 | Banana | $0.40 |
| Chicken Fingers | $2.15 | Peach | $0.35 |
| | Milk | $0.75 | |
| | Juice | $0.65 | |

1. Emma orders a hot dog, an apple, and milk. How much does she have to pay for her meal?

_____

2. Danny orders an orange. He pays with a $1 bill. How much change should he receive?

_____

3. Lucas orders chicken fingers and juice. He pays with a $5 bill. How much change should he receive?

_____

4. Ruth has $5. She orders two hamburgers. Does she have enough money left to buy a drink?

_____

5. Carl orders grilled cheese, juice, and a banana. He gives the cashier $3.00. How much change should he receive?

_____

6. Nancy orders chicken fingers, milk, and a piece of fruit. She pays $3.35 for her meal. What kind of fruit does she buy?

_____

7. The Baker family orders 3 hamburgers and 3 milks. They pay with a $10 bill. How much change should they receive?

_____

8. You have $4.00 to spend for lunch. List what you will order.

_____

_____

# Candle Clocks

A long time ago, people used candles to measure the passing of time. Candles were marked to show how far they would burn down in 1 hour. By counting the number of 1-hour sections left unburned, people knew how many hours had gone by.

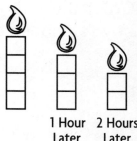

1 Hour    2 Hours
Later     Later

**1.** Write how many hours later. Then write the time.

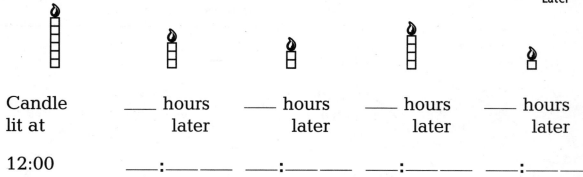

| Candle lit at | ____ hours later | ____ hours later | ____ hours later | ____ hours later |

12:00     ___:___    ___:___    ___:___    ___:___

**2.** Write the time.

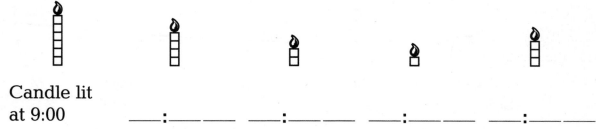

Candle lit at 9:00     ___:___    ___:___    ___:___    ___:___

**3.** Mark X's for the parts missing to show the time. The first one is done for you.

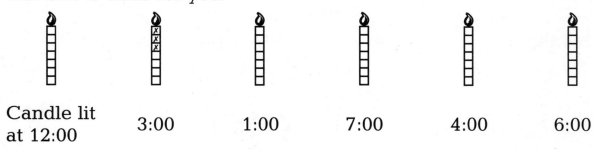

Candle lit at 12:00     3:00     1:00     7:00     4:00     6:00

**4.** What are some problems people might have had using candle clocks?

_____

_____

# Estimating How Long

Color the picture. Use the
key to choose the colors.

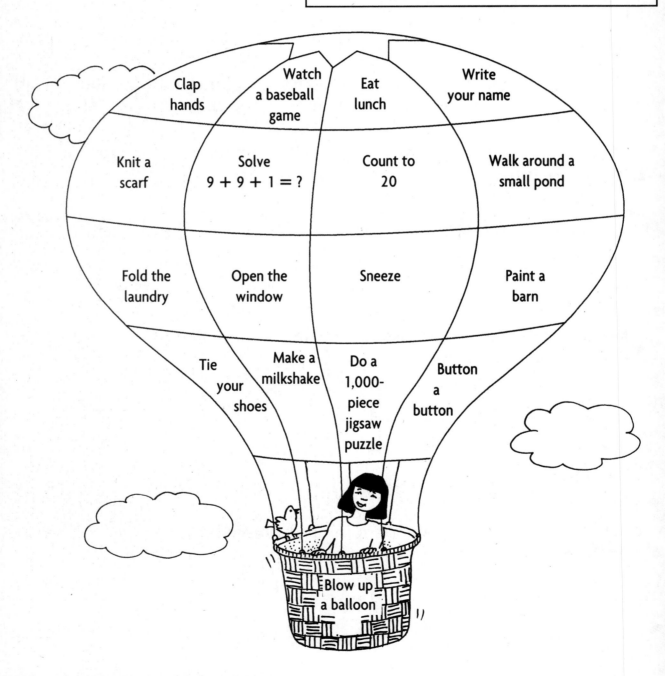

Clap hands

Watch a baseball game

Eat lunch

Write your name

Knit a scarf

Solve $9 + 9 + 1 = ?$

Count to 20

Walk around a small pond

Fold the laundry

Open the window

Sneeze

Paint a barn

Tie your shoes

Make a milkshake

Do a 1,000-piece jigsaw puzzle

Button a button

Blow up a balloon

Name _____

# Hours and Hours

If you spend about 2 hours each day eating, about how many hours do you spend eating each week? each month? each year?

**Think:**
7 days in 1 week,
about 4 weeks in 1 month,
12 months in 1 year

- To find the number of hours you spend eating in a week, multiply 2 hours times 7.

So, you spend about 14 hours eating each week.

- To find the number of hours you spend eating in a month, multiply 14 hours times 4.

So, you spend about 56 hours eating each month.

- To find the number of hours you spend eating in a year, multiply 56 hours times 12.

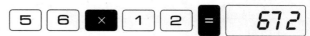

So, you spend about 672 hours eating each year.

---

Use a calculator. Complete the chart. Round times to the nearest hour. Include an activity of your own.

1.

| Activity | Number of Hours | | | |
|---|---|---|---|---|
| | **Each Day** | **Each Week** | **Each Month** | **Each Year** |
| Sleeping | | | | |
| Reading | | | | |
| Helping Out at Home | | | | |
| Playing | | | | |
| | | | | |

2. Look at the chart. What do you spend the greatest number of hours doing each year? the least number of hours?

_____

# Roman Numerals

Sometimes the numbers on a clockface are Roman numerals.

The Roman numeral for 4 is IV, but many clockmakers thought the symbol IIII looked better, so often you will see IIII instead of IV.

10:30

---

Compare the clock with Roman numerals with a regular clock. Write the number the Roman numerals represent.

**1.** II      **2.** VI      **3.** X      **4.** VII      **5.** IIII

_____  _____  _____  _____  _____

**6.** XI      **7.** V      **8.** XII      **9.** VIII      **10.** IX

_____  _____  _____  _____  _____

Write the Roman numeral that the hour hand would point to.

**11.** 1:00      **12.** 5:00      **13.** 10:00      **14.** 4:00

_____  _____  _____  _____

**15.** 11:00      **16.** 8:00      **17.** 6:00      **18.** 9:00

_____  _____  _____  _____

Write the time.

**19.**

**20.**

**21.**

_____  _____  _____

# A Riddle in Time

**7:15**

**7:30**

**7:45**

**15 minutes** after seven          **30 minutes** after seven          **15 minutes** before eight

Finish the riddle. For each time in 1–18, find in the box
below the time that matches. Write on the line the letter
in the circle.

1. 15 minutes after nine    (l)        2. 15 minutes before ten    (n)

3. 30 minutes after three   (f)        4. 30 minutes after two     (b)

5. 15 minutes before six    (s)        6. 30 minutes after ten     (o)

7. 15 minutes before nine   (u)        8. 15 minutes after six     (a)

9. 15 minutes before one    (n)        10. 30 minutes after four    (a)

11. 30 minutes after eight  (c)        12. 15 minutes before eleven (s)

13. 15 minutes before four  (e)        14. 15 minutes after three   (t)

15. 15 minutes after one    (d)        16. 15 minutes after eleven  (h)

17. 15 minutes after five   (g)        18. 30 minutes after eleven  (e)

What has a ___ ___ ___ ___ and ___ ___ ___ ___ ___
         3:30  6:15  8:30  3:45          11:15  4:30  9:45  1:15  5:45

___ ___ ___   ___ ___   ___ ___ ___ ___ ?
2:30  8:45  3:15    12:45  10:30    9:15  11:30  5:15  10:45

# A Riddle

## What do pilot rabbits fly?

Use the clocks to answer the riddle. Find the clock that matches each time written at the bottom of the page. Place the letter of the clock in the box above the time.

| A | L | S | E |
|---|---|---|---|

| N | H | P | R |
|---|---|---|---|

| | | | |
|---|---|---|---|
| 15 minutes after 9:15 | 1 hour after 7:30 | 30 minutes after 4:15 | 1 hour 15 minutes after 10:00 |

| | | | | | |
|---|---|---|---|---|---|
| 15 minutes after 9:45 | 30 minutes after 11:45 | 15 minutes after 8:15 | 45 minutes after 1:30 | 30 minutes after 10:45 | 45 minutes after 3:15 |

# What's on the Air?

1. Bill listened to the Folk Tales program. When the program was over, he played baseball for 1 hour and 15 minutes. At what time did he finish playing baseball?

_____

2. Mrs. Johnson listened to station WCAT from 7:00 to 8:30 on Saturday. How many different programs did she listen to?

_____

| WCAT SATURDAY RADIO SCHEDULE | |
| --- | --- |
| News | 7:00 |
| Weather Report | 7:45 |
| Sports Report | 8:00 |
| Story Time—Folk Tales | 8:30 |
| Music | 9:30 |
| Story Time—Animal Tales | 10:45 |
| News Update | 11:30 |
| Off the Air | 12:00 |

3. Tammy wants to listen to the Animal Tales program. It is now 10:15. How many minutes does Tammy have to wait before the program comes on the air?

_____

4. Carlos listened to the Animal Tales program. Before that, he practiced the drums for 30 minutes. At what time did he start practicing?

_____

5. How much longer are the Folk Tales than the Animal Tales?

_____

6. Which program is on the air for the longest time?

_____

7. Colleen tuned the radio to station WCAT at 10:15 on Saturday morning. What program did she hear?

_____

8. Mr. Murphy woke up at 8:00 on Saturday. What time should he tune the radio to WCAT to listen to the news?

_____

# Making a Schedule

Mr. Frank's third grade class is going on a field trip to a
nature center. Mr. Frank drew a picture of a clock to
show when each activity begins.

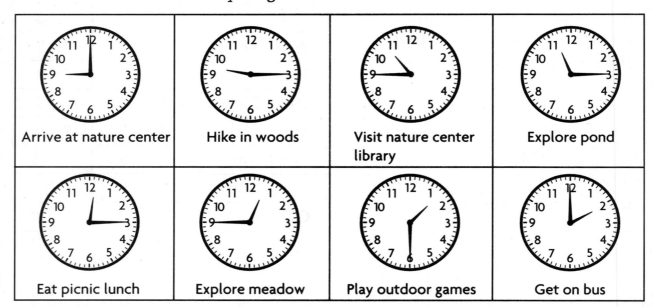

| Arrive at nature center | Hike in woods | Visit nature center library | Explore pond |
| Eat picnic lunch | Explore meadow | Play outdoor games | Get on bus |

1. Make a schedule that shows how long each activity lasts.

| Activity | Start Time | End Time | Elapsed Time |
|---|---|---|---|
| Arrive | 9:00 | 9:15 | 15 min |
| Hike | _____ | _____ | _____ |
| Visit library | _____ | _____ | _____ |
| Explore pond | _____ | _____ | _____ |
| Eat lunch | _____ | _____ | _____ |
| Explore meadow | _____ | _____ | _____ |
| Play games | _____ | _____ | _____ |

2. Which activity lasts the longest? _____

3. How much time in all will the class spend at the

   nature center? _____

# Taking Turns

Ann, Ben, Carol, and Dan take turns doing chores.
They made a schedule for the chores that they do.

1. Look for a pattern in the schedule. Then use the
   pattern to complete the schedule.

| Day | Walk Dog | Set Table | Wash Dishes |
|-----|----------|-----------|-------------|
| **Monday** | Ann | Ben | Carol |
| **Tuesday** | Dan | Ann | Ben |
| **Wednesday** | Carol | Dan | Ann |
| **Thursday** | Ben | Carol | Dan |
| **Friday** | Ann | _____ | _____ |
| **Saturday** | _____ | _____ | _____ |
| **Sunday** | _____ | _____ | _____ |

For Problems 2–6, use the schedule.

2. On what days does Ann walk
   the dog?

   _____

3. What chore does Dan do on
   Wednesday?

   _____

4. Who sets the table only one
   time during the week?

   _____

5. On what days does Ben have
   no chores?

   _____

6. Ben said that the schedule is not quite fair. Give one
   reason why Ben may have said this.

   _____

   _____

   _____

# Calendar Patterns

Sam cut out a column of numbers from his calendar.

He noticed that each number is 7 more than the number above it.

| 4 | $4 + 7 = 11$ |
| 11 | $11 + 7 = 18$ |
| 18 | $18 + 7 = 25$ |
| 25 | |

## Fill in the numbers that are missing from these calendar pieces.

**1.**

| 10 |
| |
| 24 |

**2.**

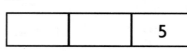

| | | 5 |

**3.**

| 1 | |
| | |

**4.**

| | |
| 19 | |

**5.**

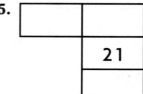

| | |
| | 21 |
| | |

**6.**

| | |
| 10 | |

**7.**

| | 2 | |
| | | |

**8.**

| | | |
| | 30 | |

**9.**

| | 15 | |
| | | |

**10.**

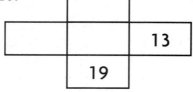

| | | |
| | 13 |
| 19 | |

**11.**

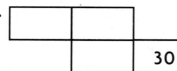

| | | |
| 10 | |
| | |

**12.**

| | | 9 |
| | | |
| | | |

# Work Forward or Backward

| July | | | | | | |
|------|------|------|------|------|------|------|
| Sun | Mon | Tue | Wed | Thu | Fri | Sat |
|  | 1 | 2 | 3 | 4 | 5 | 6 |
| 7 | 8 | 9 | 10 | 11 | 12 | 13 |
| 14 | 15 | 16 | 17 | 18 | 19 | 20 |
| 21 | 22 | 23 | 24 | 25 | 26 | 27 |
| 28 | 29 | 30 | 31 | | | |

| August | | | | | | |
|------|------|------|------|------|------|------|
| Sun | Mon | Tue | Wed | Thu | Fri | Sat |
|  |  |  |  | 1 | 2 | 3 |
| 4 | 5 | 6 | 7 | 8 | 9 | 10 |
| 11 | 12 | 13 | 14 | 15 | 16 | 17 |
| 18 | 19 | 20 | 21 | 22 | 23 | 24 |
| 25 | 26 | 27 | 28 | 29 | 30 | 31 |

1. Sam takes a piano lesson on the first and third Wednesday of every month. Sam's grandparents are coming to visit 2 days before his first piano lesson in August. On what date are Sam's grandparents coming to visit?

_____

2. The Scott family started a vacation on July 13. They drove for 3 days, stayed at the beach for 1 week, and then drove home in 2 days. On what day of the week did they return home?

_____

3. Maria's birthday is one week after July 4. She is having a birthday party on the Saturday after her birthday. On what date is Maria having her party?

_____

4. Tom finished reading a book on August 22. He spent 3 weeks reading the book. On what date did he begin reading the book?

_____

5. Danielle starts camp on the last Friday in July. She stays at camp for 2 weeks. On what date does she leave camp?

_____

6. Josh finished making a model airplane on August 12. He spent 1 week putting the model together and 2 days painting it. When did Josh start working on the model?

_____

# River Riddle

Solve the riddle. First, count the money and write each amount. Then, go to the bottom of the page. Write the letter that shows each amount. The answer will appear.

## Why is the river rich?

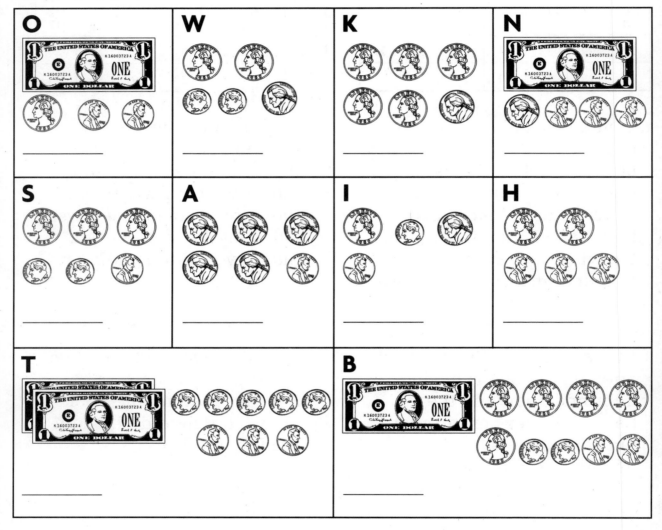

| $0.41 | $2.53 |
|---|---|
|  |  |

| $0.53 | $0.26 | $0.96 |
|---|---|---|
|  |  |  |

| $2.53 | $0.75 | $1.27 |
|---|---|---|
|  |  |  |

| $2.47 | $0.26 | $1.08 | $1.30 | $0.96 |
|---|---|---|---|---|
|  |  |  |  |  |

# Lemonade Stand

Andy is selling lemonade for
$0.50 a cup. He started a table
showing different ways to pay for
lemonade, using quarters, dimes,
and nickels.

Complete the table.

| 1. | Quarters | Dimes | Nickels |
|---|---|---|---|
| | 2 | 0 | 0 |
| | 1 | 2 | 1 |
| | | | |
| | | | |
| | | | |
| | | | |
| | | | |
| | | | |
| | | | |
| | | | |

Write how many different ways
you can pay for lemonade.

**2.** with just nickels and dimes

_____

**3.** with exactly 6 coins

_____

**4.** with an odd number of coins

_____

**5.** Jerry buys 3 cups of lemonade. How much money does
he spend?

_____

**6.** Nancy has 1 quarter, 4 dimes,
and 8 nickels. Does she have
enough money to buy 2 cups
of lemonade?

_____

**7.** Butch has $2.75. Can he buy
6 cups of lemonade?

_____

**8.** How much money would Leah
spend to buy lemonade for
herself and 4 friends?

_____

# Shopping at the Pet Store

$1.49          $0.46          $0.89          $0.33          $2.98

**1.** Jim has

Does Jim have enough money to buy a brush?

_____

**2.** Carrie has

Does Carrie have enough money to buy 2 cans of cat food?

_____

**3.** Lisa has

How much more money does Lisa need to buy a bowl?

_____

**4.** Fred has

How much money will Fred have left if he buys a can of cat food?

_____

**5.** Jane pays for a toy mouse with 8 coins. What coins does she use?

_____

_____

**6.** Paul pays for a ball with 4 coins. What coins does he use?

_____

_____

# Party Time

Complete the table of items needed to make a cake.

| Paid | Cost of Item | Change Received |
|---|---|---|
| (8 dimes) | $0.74 | |
| (2 one dollar bills) | $1.29 | |
| | $1.49 | $3.51 |
| | $0.65 | $0.35 |
| (1 one dollar bill, 1 quarter) | | $0.20 |
| (4 quarters, 1 dime) | | $0.01 |
| (2 one dollar bills, 2 quarters) | OIL | $0.15 |

# What's Missing?

Write the missing numbers.

1.
```
   $ 2 . 5  5
 +   1 . 9  8
 _____
   $ □ . 5  □
```

2.
```
   $ 2 . 9  5
 +   3 . □  9
 _____
   $ 6 . 6  4
```

3.
```
   $ 4 . 5  9
 + □ . 3  □
 _____
   $ 6 . 9  8
```

4.
```
   $ 3 . □  1
 + □ . 3  9
 _____
   $ 5 . 3  0
```

5.
```
   $ 3 . 9  5
 -   1 . 4  9
 _____
   $ □ . 4  □
```

6.
```
   $ 4 . 5  0
 -   1 . □  8
 _____
   $ 3 . 2  2
```

7.
```
   $ 6 . 5  9
 - □ . 9  □
 _____
   $ 4 . 6  7
```

8.
```
   $ 8 . □  5
 - □ . 4  9
 _____
   $ 7 . 2  6
```

For Problems 9–12, use the table.

9. Bob buys 2 peanut butter and jelly sandwiches. He gives the clerk a $5 bill. List the change he will get.

_____

| Sandwiches | |
|---|---|
| Ham | $1.89 |
| Cheese | $1.35 |
| Chicken | $2.19 |
| Peanut butter and jelly | $0.95 |

10. Joan buys a sandwich. She gives the clerk a $5 bill. Her change is $3.11. What kind of sandwich does she buy?

_____

11. How much more does a chicken sandwich cost than a cheese sandwich?

_____

12. Make up your own problem about sandwiches you will buy for yourself and a friend. Have a classmate solve it.

_____

_____

_____

_____

# Shopping Spree

$19.99        $25.50        $7.75        $15.97        $18.50

**1.** Mr. Cohen buys 2 gifts. He spends $33.25. What does he buy?

_____

**2.** Mrs. Talbot buys 2 gifts. She spends $34.47. What does she buy?

_____

**3.** Mrs. Chan buys 2 gifts. She spends less than $25.00. What does she buy?

_____

**4.** Mr. McDonald pays for a watch with a $10 bill and two $5 bills. What is his change?

_____

**5.** Mrs. Park buys one gift. Her change from a $20 bill is $4.03. What does she buy?

_____

**6.** Mr. Brooks buys one gift. His change from two $20 bills is $14.50. What does he buy?

_____

**7.** Sam wants to buy a watch. He has saved $15.25. How much more money does he need to buy the watch?

_____

**8.** Sarah got $25.00 for her birthday. If she buys a bear, how much money will she have left?

_____

**9.** Make up your own problem about the gifts that are shown. Have a classmate solve it.

_____

_____

_____

# Circus Time

The circus is coming to town! A circus train is carrying animals in 5 wagons. The bear is behind the pony. The bear is ahead of the elephant. The dog is ahead of the lion. The bear is in the fourth wagon.

1. Which animal is in the first wagon? _____

2. Which animal is in the second wagon? _____

Six boys are in line to buy tickets for the circus. Jon is behind Tim. Pedro is ahead of Carl. Leon is between Jon and Pedro. There are 4 boys between Sam and Carl. Jon is third in line.

3. Who is last in line? _____

4. Who is first in line? _____

5. Who is second in line? _____

# Trade to Win

Work with a partner.

**Materials:**

- 2 number cubes with numbers 1–6
- 30 pennies, 30 dimes, and a $1 bill
- Game grids for each player

**How to Play:**

The object of the game is to get the $1 bill.

One of the players is the banker for each game. That person gives out and trades the money.

Take turns. Roll both number cubes, and add the numbers that come up. Take the number of pennies equal to the sum.

Whenever a player gets 10 pennies, he or she trades them at the bank for 1 dime. Mark an X in a box for each dime you get. When you have marked 10 X's, trade for the $1 bill. The first player to get the $1 bill is the banker for the next game.

| Game 1 | | | | | | | | | |
|--------|--|--|--|--|--|--|--|--|--|
| Dimes | | | | | | | | | |

| Game 2 | | | | | | | | | |
|--------|--|--|--|--|--|--|--|--|--|
| Dimes | | | | | | | | | |

| Game 3 | | | | | | | | | |
|--------|--|--|--|--|--|--|--|--|--|
| Dimes | | | | | | | | | |

# Odd-and-Even Game

Work with a partner.

**Materials:**

- Number chart shown below
- Number cube with numbers 1–6
- 30 game markers (15 each of two colors)

**How to Play:**

The object of the game is to get 5 of your markers in a row in any direction—horizontal, vertical, or diagonal.

Take turns. Roll the number cube. If the number is even, place a marker on any even number on the number chart. If the number is odd, place a marker on any odd number on the number chart.

| 1  | 2  | 3  | 4  | 5  | 6  | 7  | 8  | 9  | 10 |
|----|----|----|----|----|----|----|----|----|----|
| 11 | 12 | 13 | 14 | 15 | 16 | 17 | 18 | 19 | 20 |
| 21 | 22 | 23 | 24 | 25 | 26 | 27 | 28 | 29 | 30 |
| 31 | 32 | 33 | 34 | 35 | 36 | 37 | 38 | 39 | 40 |
| 41 | 42 | 43 | 44 | 45 | 46 | 47 | 48 | 49 | 50 |

# Number Sleuth

Here are some pieces that have been cut out of a hundred chart. Fill in the missing numbers without looking at a hundred chart. When you finish, use a hundred chart to check your answers.

1.
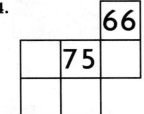

2.
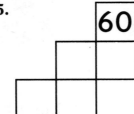

3.
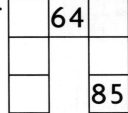

4.

5.

6.

Fill in the numbers that are neighbors of 25.

7.

8.

9.

10.

11.

12.

13.

14.

Name _____

# It's the Berries!

10 strawberries

25 blackberries

100 blueberries

For Exercises 1–10, use the benchmark numbers from the examples above. Estimate the number of berries in each container.

**1.**

_____
strawberries

**2.**

_____
blueberries

**3.**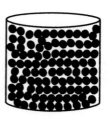

_____
blackberries

**4.**

_____
strawberries

**5.**

_____
blackberries

**6.**

_____
blueberries

**7.**

_____
blackberries

**8.**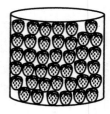

_____
strawberries

**9.** About how many strawberries would there be in 2 full containers?

_____

_____

**10.** About how many blueberries would there be in 2 full containers?

_____

_____

# How Many Marbles?

Mr. Shaw sells marbles at his toy store. He wants to
know about how many marbles of each color he has
left. How can he estimate the number of marbles left
in each jar without counting every single marble?

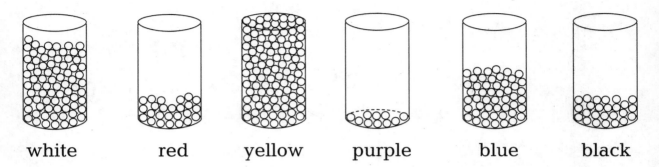

| white | red | yellow | purple | blue | black |

Mr. Shaw can make a model.
He finds an empty jar the same
size. He chooses the benchmark
number 25 and puts 25 marbles
into the jar.

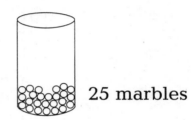

25 marbles

Use the benchmark model to estimate the number of
marbles left in each color.

**1.** white _____

**2.** red _____

**3.** yellow _____

**4.** purple _____

**5.** blue _____

**6.** black _____

**7.** The jar of blue marbles was
full at the beginning of the
month. About how many blue
marbles has Mr. Shaw sold
this month?

**8.** About how many more yellow
marbles are left than black
marbles?

_____

_____

# Colorful Balloons

Read the clues. Color the balloons.

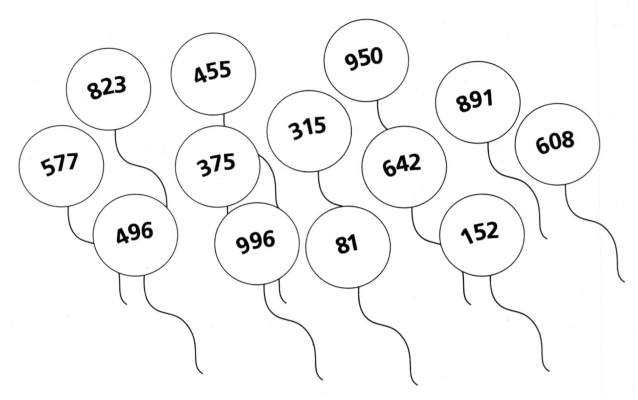

1. A balloon with a two in the ones place is red.

2. If the balloon has a one in the tens place,
   color it blue.

3. A balloon whose number equals 175 + 200 is yellow.

4. The smallest-numbered balloon is green.

5. Color the balloon with a zero in the ones place purple.

6. The largest-numbered balloon is brown.

7. Any balloon whose number is 576 + 1 is orange.

8. A balloon with an eight in the hundreds place
   is black.

9. If the balloon has a zero in the tens place,
   color it pink.

10. If the number is 555 − 100, color the balloon gray.

# Number Search

**Daily Newspaper**

Section A, pages 1–15

Section B, pages 16–27

Section C, pages 28–45

**Storybook**

pages 1–1,000

**Capitol Building**

152 Bradford Rd.

**Dictionary**

Letter C, pages 62–110

**Houses**

301–311 Main St.

## Use the clues above to answer the following questions.

1. Can you find page 14 of the newspaper in Section B?

_____

2. On what page in the dictionary does letter *D* begin?

_____

3. Can you see a house at 314 Main St.?

_____

4. I am reading page 978. What am I reading?

_____

5. Can you find the word *cookie* on page 29 in the dictionary?

_____

6. What is the address of the capitol building?

_____

7. Write three page numbers you can find in the storybook.

_____

# Secret Message

Solve the problems. Find the letter that goes with the
answer and put it in the blank. When you have finished,
you will have found the secret message.

| $\dfrac{O}{900}$ | $\dfrac{E}{3,700}$ | $\dfrac{A}{200}$ | $\dfrac{Y}{500}$ | $\dfrac{T}{450}$ |
|---|---|---|---|---|
| $\dfrac{S}{600}$ | $\dfrac{V}{1,082}$ | $\dfrac{M}{950}$ | $\dfrac{R}{2,050}$ | $\dfrac{U}{1,000}$ |

_____     _____     _____

200 + 300     400 + 500     2,000 − 1,000

_____     _____     _____

600 − 400     1,050 + 1,000     3,500 + 200

_____     _____     _____     _____

1,382 − 300     3,900 − 200     2,450 − 400     800 − 300

_____   _____   _____   _____   _____!

400 + 200   150 + 800   900 − 700   2,000 + 50   250 + 200

Use the code to make up your own message. Share
your message with a friend.

# Matching Numbers

Match the correct number to the written form of
the number.

1. eighty-three thousand,
   nine hundred seventy-six

   **A.** 14,619

2. ninety-four thousand,
   three hundred four

   **B.** 94,304

3. sixty-two thousand,
   five hundred ten

   **C.** 75,826

4. seventy-five thousand,
   eight hundred twenty-six

   **D.** 35,247

5. forty-seven thousand,
   four hundred eight

   **E.** 83,976

6. thirty-five thousand,
   two hundred forty-seven

   **F.** 66,152

7. fourteen thousand,
   six hundred nineteen

   **G.** 42,706

8. sixty-six thousand,
   one hundred fifty-two

   **H.** 62,510

9. twenty-eight thousand,
   nine hundred eighty-three

   **I.** 47,408

10. forty-two thousand,
    seven hundred six

    **J.** 28,983

# Missing Numbers

Detective Casey needs to find some missing numbers. Can
you help her? When you find them, circle the numbers
so she knows where to look. The numbers can be found
going up, across, down, backward, and diagonally.

```
1   2   8   6   7   4   3   0   5
5   0   1   9   4   2   1   8   9
2   2   7   8   0   1   3   6   4
4   8   7   5   2   6   0   4   3
7   5   1   4   6   2   1   0   8
4   6   9   8   2   0   3   4   7
0   8   5   2   4   3   0   1   6
2   9   3   7   4   6   5   0   9
1   7   2   8   3   9   6   4   5
```

| | | |
|---|---|---|
| 1. 17,283 | 2. 50,194 | 3. 3,756 |
| 4. 27,423 | 5. 44,104 | 6. 4,301 |
| 7. 9,820 | 8. 5,469 | 9. 94,387 |
| 10. 9,132 | 11. 6,150 | 12. 7,402 |
| 13. 31,301 | 14. 28,674 | 15. 5,820 |

Detective Casey thanks you for all your hard work in
helping her find the missing numbers.

# Table Talk

Carl's Pen Store expects a
busy year. The table shows
how many pens Carl has
in his store.

| Carl's Pen Store | |
|---|---|
| Blue | 29,492 |
| Red | 13,650 |
| Green | 9,834 |
| Black | 6,500 |
| Purple | 2,173 |

For Problems 1–8, use
the table to solve.

1. Carl mails all his blue pens
to California. He can only fit
10,000 pens in a box. How
many boxes will he need?

_____

2. Eric needs 2,000 green pens
and 1,000 red pens. How
many pens does he need
in all?

_____

3. Tony orders 2,000 of the
purple pens. Carl mails them
in groups of 1,000. How
many groups does Carl mail
to Tony?

_____

4. Amy needs to buy 7,000 black
pens. She goes to Carl's store
and buys all his black pens.
How many pens does she still
need to buy?

_____

5. Michelle buys 1,000 red pens.
How many red pens does
Carl have left?

_____

6. Carl has about 10,000 pens of
which color?

_____

7. If Carl sells all his green,
black, and purple pens, how
many pens will he sell in all?

_____

8. Which color pens can be
mailed in boxes of 10,000?

_____

# Model Numbers

Look at the models below. Under each, write the number
that the model represents. When you finish, follow the
directions at the bottom of the page.

○ = hundreds      ☆ = tens      □ = ones

**1.** ☆ ☆ ☆ ☆
□ □ □ □

_____

**2.** ☆ ☆ ☆
□ □

_____

**3.** ☆ ☆ ☆
□

_____

**4.** ☆ ☆ ☆ ☆ ☆
□ □ □

_____

**5.** ☆ ☆ ☆ ☆
□ □ □ □ □ □

_____

**6.** ☆ ☆
□ □

_____

**7.** ○ ○ ○
☆ ☆
□ □ □

_____

**8.** ○ ○ ○
☆ ☆ ☆
□ □

_____

**9.** ○ ○ ○
☆ ☆ ☆
□ □

_____

**10.** In Exercises 1–9, circle the
answer that is the greatest
number.

**11.** In Exercises 1–9, what is the
number that is closest to the
greatest number in size?

_____

**12.** In Exercises 1–9, put a square
around the answer that is the
smallest number.

**13.** In Exercises 1–9, what is the
number that is closest to the
smallest number in size?

_____

**14.** Choose your own number. Write what that
number is, and model it by using circles,
stars, and squares.

_____

# Seven Roads

Erica lives where seven roads meet. Look at the map, and then answer the questions below.

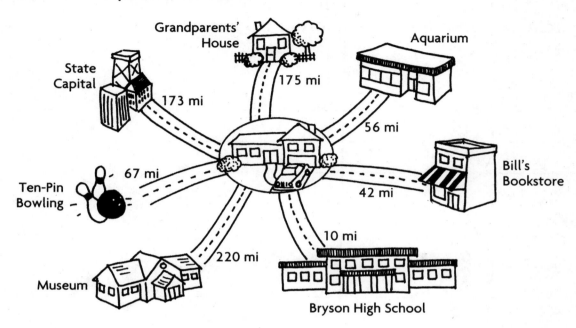

1. Which place on the map is farthest from Erica's house?

_____

2. Which place on the map is closest to Erica's house?

_____

3. How much farther is the aquarium than the high school from Erica's house?

_____

4. Is it farther from Erica's house to the state capital or from Erica's house to the bookstore and back?

_____

5. Is it a farther drive from Erica's house to the bowling alley and back, or from Erica's house to her grandparents' house?

_____

6. If Erica drives to all the places on the map, starting and ending at home, how far will she drive? (Remember, she has to go back to her house each time.)

_____

# Scrambled Numbers!

Pick numbers from each circle to make 3 different three-digit numbers. Write your numbers on the lines to the left of the circle. Then, on the lines to the right of the circle, put your numbers in order from least to greatest.

1. _____ 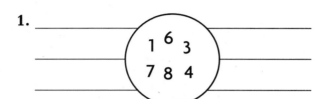 _____

2. _____ 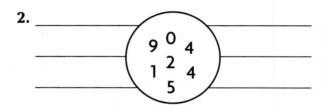 _____

3. _____ 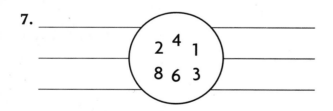 _____

4. _____ 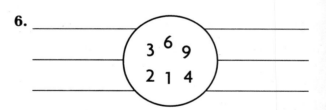 _____

5. _____ 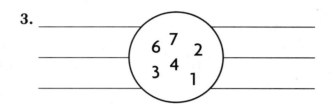 _____

6. _____ 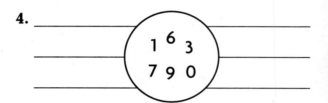 _____

7. _____ 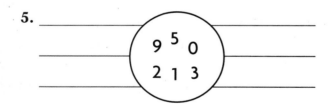 _____

8. _____ 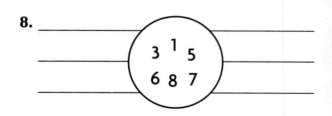 _____

9. What is the greatest number you came up with?

_____

10. What is the second greatest number you came up with?

_____

11. What is the smallest number you came up with?

_____

12. What is the second smallest number you came up with?

_____

# Drawing Fun

Work with a partner to draw number lines for the
problems below. Then solve.

1. You and your friend go to the
   store and buy a game for
   $14, a calculator for $12, and
   a video for $15. Which item is
   the least expensive?

   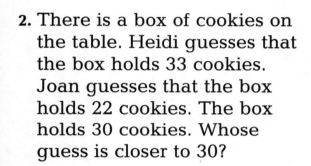

   _____

2. There is a box of cookies on
   the table. Heidi guesses that
   the box holds 33 cookies.
   Joan guesses that the box
   holds 22 cookies. The box
   holds 30 cookies. Whose
   guess is closer to 30?

   _____

3. Sonya has three cans of soup:
   8, 16, and 32 ounces. Which
   can of soup is the smallest?

   _____

You and your partner write a word problem using the
picture on the right. Then solve each other's problem.

4. _____

   _____

   _____

   _____

   _____

# Round and Round We Go!

Look at the table at the bottom of the page. Round the two-digit numbers to the nearest ten and the three-digit numbers to the nearest hundred. Then find the heart or hearts that have the rounded number. Use the table to color them.

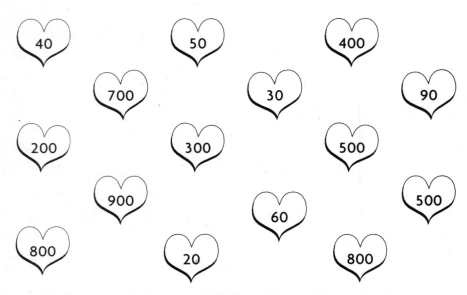

| Number | Rounded Number | Color |
|--------|----------------|-------|
| 25 | | red |
| 167 | | blue |
| 334 | | green |
| 63 | | yellow |
| 751 | | purple |
| 888 | | orange |
| 85 | | brown |
| 378 | | pink |
| 47 | | gray |
| 18 | | black |
| 457 | | dark blue |
| 696 | | light green |
| 39 | | turquoise |

# Quick Sale

George's General Merchandise is having a sale. Each sale table will hold items that have been rounded to the nearest ten or hundred for a quick sale. Under each item, write the table it should go on.

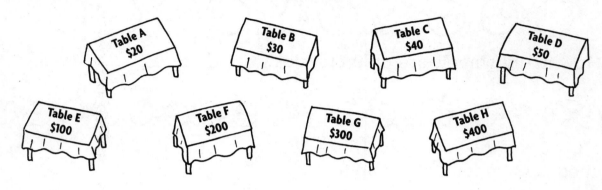

Table A $20  Table B $30  Table C $40  Table D $50

Table E $100  Table F $200  Table G $300  Table H $400

**1.**

$189

_____

**2.**

$25

_____

**3.**

$175

_____

**4.**

$23

_____

**5.**

$187

_____

**6.**

$259

_____

**7.**

$37

_____

**8.**

$157

_____

**9.**

$313

_____

**10.**

$45

_____

**11.**

$44

_____

**12.**

$113

_____

# Making Equal Groups

The prefix *bi-* means *two*. A *bi*cycle has two wheels.

**1.** How many wheels are on 5 bicycles? _____

**2.** How many wheels are on 9 bicycles? _____

A *bi*ped is an animal with two feet.

**3.** How many feet do 4 bipeds have? _____

**4.** How many feet do 7 bipeds have? _____

Something that happens every two months is *bi*monthly.

**5.** Alice subscribes to a bimonthly magazine. She received the first issue in February. When will Alice receive the next three issues?

_____

**6.** Todd makes bimonthly visits to a museum. His first visit was in May. When will Todd make his next three visits?

_____

# Pattern Plot

Find the next three numbers.
Write the rule used to make the pattern.

1. 22, 24, 26, 28, _____, _____, _____

   Rule: _____

2. 80, 85, 90, 95, _____, _____, _____

   Rule: _____

3. 117, 122, 127, 132, _____, _____, _____

   Rule: _____

4. 211, 213, 215, 217, _____, _____, _____

   Rule: _____

5. 317, 319, 324, 326, 331, _____, _____, _____

   Rule: _____

6. 89, 94, 99, 101, 106, 111, 113, _____, _____, _____

   Rule: _____

Make up your own pattern using differences of 2 or 5, or both. Write your rule under your pattern.

7. _____ _____ _____ _____ _____ _____ _____

   Rule: _____

8. _____ _____ _____ _____ _____ _____ _____

   Rule: _____

# Floor Fun

You have been asked to design a colorful ballroom dancing floor. The floor is 10 tiles wide and 12 tiles long, so it contains 120 tiles.

The ballroom owner tells you to use <u>5 times as many green tiles as blue tiles</u>, <u>2 times as many yellow tiles as orange tiles</u>, and <u>2 times as many purple tiles as red tiles</u>. He tells you that <u>you can also use white tiles</u> in your design.

How many tiles of each color will you use? Write your answers below. Make sure you use 120 tiles in all. Then color in your design.

_____ green    _____ yellow    _____ purple    _____ white

_____ blue    _____ orange    _____ red

# Puzzling Products

Find the product for each Column 1 problem in Column 2.
Then write the product's circled letter on the line in front
of the problem.

**Column 1**

_____ **1.** $9 \times 3$

_____ **2.** $5 \times 5$

_____ **3.** $2 \times 4$

_____ **4.** $7 \times 3$

_____ **5.** $3 \times 5$

_____ **6.** $8 \times 2$

_____ **7.** $6 \times 3$

_____ **8.** $2 \times 5$

_____ **9.** $3 \times 8$

_____ **10.** $5 \times 6$

_____ **11.** $2 \times 3$

**Column 2**

(A) 18

(B) 8

(D) 24

(E) 15

(M) 10

(N) 27

(O) 6

(R) 30

(S) 25

(U) 16

(Y) 21

Use your answers to decode the sentence below. The
problem number under each blank tells you where to look
in Column 1. Write on the sentence blank the letter that
is in front of the problem number.

___ ___ ___ ___ ___ ___ ___     ___ ___ ___
7   9   9   5   1   9   2      7   10  5

___ ___ ___ ___ ___ ___ ___     ___ ___ ___     ___ ___ ___ .
1   6   8   3   5   10  2      4   11  6       7   9   9

# Fit Feasting Facts

The Food Guide Pyramid is a guide to healthy eating. It shows how to build a healthy diet by eating different kinds of foods.

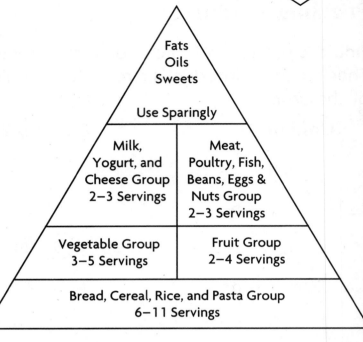

Fats
Oils
Sweets

Use Sparingly

Milk, Yogurt, and Cheese Group
2–3 Servings

Meat, Poultry, Fish, Beans, Eggs & Nuts Group
2–3 Servings

Vegetable Group
3–5 Servings

Fruit Group
2–4 Servings

Bread, Cereal, Rice, and Pasta Group
6–11 Servings

Use the Food Guide Pyramid to answer the questions below.

1. How many servings of fruit should you eat every day?

_____

2. How many servings of bread, cereal, rice, and pasta should you eat every day?

_____

3. Every day, Max eats the most servings of vegetables recommended by the Food Guide Pyramid. How many servings of vegetables does Max eat in a week?

_____

4. Every day, Julie eats the fewest servings of bread, cereal, rice, and pasta recommended by the Food Guide Pyramid. How many servings from this group does Julie eat in 3 days?

_____

5. Every day, Juan eats the least number of servings from the milk, yogurt, and cheese group shown in the pyramid. How many servings of this group does Juan eat in 5 days?

_____

6. Tamala eats the greatest number of servings of the meat, poultry, fish, beans, eggs, and nuts group every day. How many servings of this group does she eat in 8 days?

_____

# Pondering Products

Find the product for each Column 1 problem in Column 2.
Then write the product's circled letter on the line in front
of the problem.

| Column 1 | Column 2 |
|---|---|
| _____ 1. $4 \times 9$ | (E) 8 |
| _____ 2. $3 \times 2$ | (F) 0 |
| _____ 3. $2 \times 8$ | (I) 36 |
| _____ 4. $0 \times 4$ | (X) 45 |
| _____ 5. $8 \times 4$ | (M) 40 |
| _____ 6. $5 \times 7$ | (N) 20 |
| _____ 7. $4 \times 2$ | (O) 16 |
| _____ 8. $2 \times 7$ | (R) 32 |
| _____ 9. $5 \times 9$ | (S) 14 |
| _____ 10. $8 \times 5$ | (T) 6 |
| _____ 11. $5 \times 4$ | (U) 35 |

Use your answers to decode the sentence below. The
problem number under each blank tells you where to look
in Column 1. Write on the sentence blank the letter that
is in front of the problem number.

___ ___ ___ ___    ___ ___ ___ ___ ___        ___ ___ ___ ___
 4   3   6   5      2   1   10  7   8           4   3   6   5

___ ___    ___ ___ ___ ___ ___ ___ ___ .
 1   8      8   1   9   2   7   7   11

# The Array Game

Play alone or with a partner.

**Materials:** 10 × 10 grid, two number cubes for each player, crayons or colored pencils

**How to Play:**

- Roll the number cubes. If you are playing with a partner, take turns rolling.

- Color in a rectangle (or square) on your grid with a length and width that correspond to the numbers you rolled.

  **Example:** Suppose you roll [dice showing 2] and [dice showing 6].

  Color in a rectangle that is 2 squares wide and 6 squares long or 6 squares wide and 2 squares long. You may place the rectangle anywhere you wish on your grid.

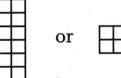

- Keep playing to color in the entire grid or until you get stuck. You are stuck when you cannot fit a rectangle anywhere on your grid.

**Score:** Your score is the total number of squares that you have colored in by the time you get stuck.

**Game 1**

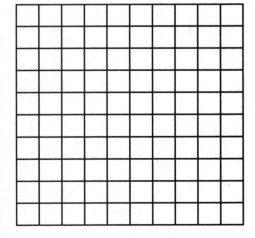

Score is _____

**Game 2**

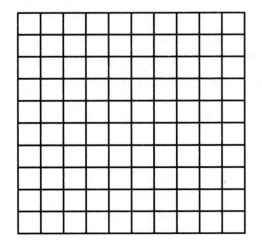

Score is _____

# Finding Factor Pairs

**What kind of fruit is always grumpy?**

To find out, draw a line to match each clue to the correct factor pair. Write the factor pair's code letter above the clue number at the bottom of page.

**Code Letter**

1. Their product is equal to 15 + 15.

              4,6     A

              6,7     P

2. Their product is odd.
   Their difference is 2.

3. Their product is equal to 3 × 8.

              4,8     S

              5,6     C

4. Their product is between 40 and 50.
   Their sum is even.

              4,7     A

5. Their product is equal to 14 + 14.

              7,9     R

6. Their product is about 40.
   Their difference is 1.

              7,8     L

7. Their product is between 35 and 40.

              3,7     E

8. Their product is greater than 50.
   Their difference is 1.

              6,6     P

9. Their product is equal to 28 − 7.

              6,8     B

10. Their product is even.
    Their difference is 4.

____ ____ ____ ____    ____ ____ ____ ____ ____ ____

  1.    2.    3.    4.       5.    6.    7.    8.    9.    10.

# Number Patterns

1. On the number chart below, put a triangle around the numbers that are multiples of 4.

2. Circle all the numbers that are multiples of 6.

3. Shade in all the numbers that are multiples of 8.

4. List the numbers that have triangles around them

   and also are circled and shaded. _____

5. Are there any shaded numbers that do not have

   triangles around them? _____

| 1 | 2 | 3 | 4 | 5 | 6 | 7 | 8 | 9 | 10 |
|---|---|---|---|---|---|---|---|---|---|
| 11 | 12 | 13 | 14 | 15 | 16 | 17 | 18 | 19 | 20 |
| 21 | 22 | 23 | 24 | 25 | 26 | 27 | 28 | 29 | 30 |
| 31 | 32 | 33 | 34 | 35 | 36 | 37 | 38 | 39 | 40 |
| 41 | 42 | 43 | 44 | 45 | 46 | 47 | 48 | 49 | 50 |
| 51 | 52 | 53 | 54 | 55 | 56 | 57 | 58 | 59 | 60 |
| 61 | 62 | 63 | 64 | 65 | 66 | 67 | 68 | 69 | 70 |
| 71 | 72 | 73 | 74 | 75 | 76 | 77 | 78 | 79 | 80 |

## Complete the equations.

6. _____ × 8 = 24     7. _____ × 8 = 48     8. _____ × 8 = 32

9. _____ × 6 = 24     10. _____ × 6 = 48     11. _____ × 6 = 30

# Multiplication Game

Play with a partner.

**Materials:** Game board below, two small paper clips, 15 to 20 game tokens for each player (each player has a different color)

**How to Play:**

- Player 1 places paper clips on two numbers at the bottom of the page. (Players may place both paper clips on the same number.) The player then multiplies the numbers and places a game token on the product.

- Player 2 moves **just one** of the paper clips to another number, multiplies the two numbers, and places a game token on the product.

- Players continue to take turns. The winner is the first player to get four game tokens in a row, column, or diagonal.

| 1 | 2 | 3 | 4 | 5 | 6 |
|---|---|---|---|---|---|
| 7 | 8 | 9 | 10 | 12 | 14 |
| 15 | 16 | 18 | 20 | 21 | 24 |
| 25 | 27 | 28 | 30 | 32 | 35 |
| 36 | 40 | 42 | 45 | 48 | 49 |
| 54 | 56 | 63 | 64 | 72 | 81 |

| 1 | 2 | 3 | 4 | 5 | 6 | 7 | 8 | 9 |
|---|---|---|---|---|---|---|---|---|

# Toothpick Shapes

You can make shapes using toothpicks.

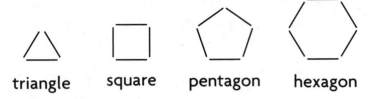

triangle     square     pentagon     hexagon

1. Complete the table to show the number of toothpicks needed to make different shapes.

| Shapes | Number of Toothpicks Needed |
|---|---|
| 3 triangles | _____ |
| 3 hexagons | _____ |
| 6 pentagons | _____ |
| 5 squares and 4 pentagons | _____ |
| _____ hexagons | 30 |
| _____ squares | 36 |
| 3 triangles and _____ pentagons | 49 |

2. List at least four different ways you can use exactly 24 toothpicks to make triangles, squares, pentagons, or hexagons. You may list shapes that are all the same or combinations of different shapes.

_____       _____

_____       _____

_____       _____

# Making Shapes

Find each product. Write the products in the multiplication table. If all of the products are correct, you will see a figure. Name the figure.

**Remember:** The first factor is the row and the second factor is the column.

| | |
|---|---|
| 7 × 4 | 8 × 4 |
| 7 × 6 | 6 × 6 |
| 6 × 5 | 8 × 6 |
| 8 × 5 | 6 × 4 |

Figure: _____

columns

| × | 1 | 2 | 3 | 4 | 5 | 6 | 7 | 8 | 9 |
|---|---|---|---|---|---|---|---|---|---|
| 1 | | | | | | | | | |
| 2 | | | | | | | | | |
| 3 | | | | | | | | | |
| 4 | | | | | | | | | |
| 5 | | | | | | | | | |
| 6 | | | | | | | | | |
| 7 | | | | | | | | | |
| 8 | | | | | | | | | |
| 9 | | | | | | | | | |

rows

# Paintbrush Division

The jars in each row need to be filled with the same number of paintbrushes. Draw the paintbrushes in each jar and complete the number sentence.

**1.**

Total number of paintbrushes: 12

Paintbrushes in each jar: _____

$12 \div 3 =$ _____

**2.**

Total number of paintbrushes: 8

Paintbrushes in each jar: _____

$8 \div 4 =$ _____

**3.**

Total number of paintbrushes: 12

Paintbrushes in each jar: _____

$12 \div 2 =$ _____

**4.**

Total number of paintbrushes: 15

Paintbrushes in each jar: _____

$15 \div 5 =$ _____

**5.**

Total number of paintbrushes: 18

Paintbrushes in each jar: _____

$18 \div 3 =$ _____

**6.**

Total number of paintbrushes: 20

Paintbrushes in each jar: _____

$20 \div 4 =$ _____

Complete the chart.

| | Number of Paintbrushes | Number of Jars | Number of Paintbrushes in Each Jar |
|---|---|---|---|
| **7.** | 24 | 4 | |
| **8.** | 21 | 3 | |
| **9.** | 30 | 5 | |

# Animal Division

Separate the animals into groups. Draw a circle around each
group. Then complete the number sentence.

**1.** 4 cats in each group

$8 \div 4 =$ _____

**2.** 3 dogs in each group

$9 \div 3 =$ _____

**3.** 3 birds in each group

$12 \div 3 =$ _____

**4.** 5 turtles in each group

$10 \div 5 =$ _____

**5.** 5 mice in each group

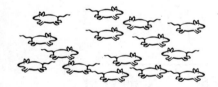

$15 \div 5 =$ _____

**6.** 3 fish in each group

$18 \div 3 =$ _____

Complete the chart.

|  | Number of Animals | Number in Each Group | Number of Groups |
|---|---|---|---|
| **7.** | 18 puppies | 3 | |
| **8.** | 20 kittens | 4 | |
| **9.** | 24 gerbils | 6 | |
| **10.** | 30 guinea pigs | 5 | |

# Missing Numbers

Complete each of the tables.

1.

| Number of Students | Number of Hands |
|---|---|
| 1 | 2 |
| 4 | |
| 6 | |
| 2 | |
| | 18 |
| | 14 |
| | 10 |

2.

| Number of Tricycles | Number of Wheels |
|---|---|
| 1 | 3 |
| 3 | |
| 7 | |
| 6 | |
| | 27 |
| | 12 |
| | 24 |

3.

| Number of 4-Leaf Clovers | Number of Leaves |
|---|---|
| 1 | 4 |
| | 12 |
| | 20 |
| | 16 |
| 9 | |
| 2 | |
| 8 | |

4.

| Number of Ants | Number of Legs |
|---|---|
| 1 | 6 |
| | 12 |
| | 30 |
| | 18 |
| 4 | |
| 7 | |
| 8 | |

# Fact Family Patterns

**1.** Fill in the missing numbers in the first three rows of
the Fact Table to complete each number sentence.

| Fact Table | | | |
|---|---|---|---|
| 18 ÷ 2 = ___ | 3 × 6 = ___ | 24 ÷ 8 = ___ | 6 × 4 = ___ |
| 6 × ___ = 18 | 24 ÷ 3 = ___ | 4 × ___ = 24 | 9 × ___ = 18 |
| 3 × ___ = 24 | 24 ÷ ___ = 6 | 2 × ___ = 18 | 18 ÷ 6 = ___ |
| _____ | _____ | _____ | _____ |

**2.** Use the colors shown below to color all the facts in
the Fact Table above that belong to each fact family.

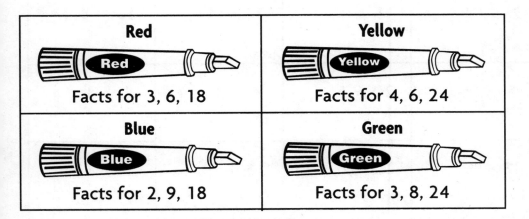

| Red | Yellow |
|---|---|
| Red | Yellow |
| Facts for 3, 6, 18 | Facts for 4, 6, 24 |
| **Blue** | **Green** |
| Blue | Green |
| Facts for 2, 9, 18 | Facts for 3, 8, 24 |

**3.** Notice the color pattern in the Fact Table, and notice
that each fact family is missing a fact. Write the
missing fact from each fact family in the bottom row
of the Fact Table. Arrange the facts so that the color
pattern continues.

# Divide to Win

Play with a partner.

**Materials:**
Game board, one number cube, 18 game markers for
each player (a different color for each player)

**How to Play:**
Players take turns as rollers and checkers. The roller rolls the
number cube and places the marker on any unmarked problem
whose quotient is the same as the number rolled.

The checker multiplies to check the roller's work. If the
answer is correct, the marker stays. If the answer is
incorrect, the marker is removed. In either case the
players then switch roles.

The winner is the first player to get four markers in
a row, a column, or a diagonal line.

| 12 ÷ 4 | 4 ÷ 1 | 18 ÷ 3 | 4 ÷ 2 | 6 ÷ 6 |
|--------|-------|--------|-------|-------|
| 15 ÷ 3 | 24 ÷ 4 | 15 ÷ 5 | 20 ÷ 4 | 16 ÷ 4 |
| 12 ÷ 6 | 5 ÷ 5 | 20 ÷ 5 | 4 ÷ 4 | 6 ÷ 3 |
| 30 ÷ 5 | 18 ÷ 6 | 30 ÷ 6 | 36 ÷ 6 | 3 ÷ 1 |
| 3 ÷ 3 | 5 ÷ 1 | 24 ÷ 6 | 8 ÷ 4 | 8 ÷ 2 |
| 10 ÷ 2 | 10 ÷ 5 | 12 ÷ 2 | 2 ÷ 2 | 6 ÷ 2 |

# The Bargain Shop

 1¢    2¢   3¢

 4¢   6¢   8¢

Write how many of each item you could buy with 24¢.

1. _____ balloons   2. _____ hats   3. _____ pencils

4. _____ buttons   5. _____ marbles   6. _____ dice

7. John bought 4 hats. How much money did he spend?

_____

8. Tracy bought 4 dice and 4 marbles. How much money did she spend?

_____

9. Bill bought 7 items that were all the same. He spent 21¢. What did he buy?

_____

10. Carlos bought 5 items that were all the same. He spent 20¢. What did he buy?

_____

11. Freddie bought 3 pencils and 2 buttons. How much money did he spend?

_____

12. Tova spent 18¢ on 9 items that were all the same. What did she buy?

_____

13. List three different ways that you could spend exactly 30¢. The items that you buy can all be the same, or they can be different.

_____

_____

_____

# Number Sentences

Complete the division and multiplication sentences that
can be used to solve each problem.

| Problem | Division Sentence | Multiplication Sentence |
|---|---|---|
| 1. There are 12 kittens.<br>There are 3 kittens in each basket.<br>How many baskets are there in all? | $12 \div 3 =$ _____ | _____ $\times 3 = 12$ |
| 2. There are 15 chairs.<br>There are 5 equal rows of chairs.<br>How many chairs are there in each row? | $15 \div 5 =$ _____ | $5 \times$ _____ $= 15$ |

Write a division sentence that can be used to solve each
problem. Then write a related multiplication sentence.

| Problem | Division Sentence | Multiplication Sentence |
|---|---|---|
| 3. There are 18 children.<br>There are 3 equal groups.<br>How many are there in each group? | _____ | _____ |
| 4. There are 15 postcards.<br>There is 1 postcard on a page.<br>How many pages have postcards? | _____ | _____ |
| 5. There are 20 mice.<br>There are 4 cages, with the<br>same number of mice in each cage.<br>How many mice are in each cage? | _____ | _____ |
| 6. There are 24 wheels.<br>How many cars are there? | _____ | _____ |
| 7. There are 16 eyes.<br>How many people are there? | _____ | _____ |

# How Does Your Garden Grow?

1. You want to plant a garden covering 12 ☐ 's. Use the grid below to draw 3 different gardens. Each one must be a rectangle with a different length and width than the other two. Then, write two division sentences about each rectangle.

| Division Sentences |
|---|
| 2. |
| |
| 3. |
| |
| 4. |
| |

5. You want to plant a garden covering 24 ☐ 's. Use the grid below to draw 4 different gardens. Each one must be a rectangle with a different length and width than the other three. Then, write two division sentences about each rectangle.

| Division Sentences |
|---|
| 6. |
| |
| 7. |
| |
| 8. |
| |
| 9. |
| |

10. Complete the table.

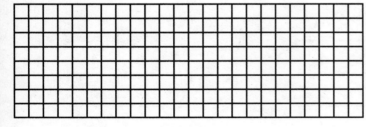

| Number of Plants | Number of Rows | Number in Each Row |
|---|---|---|
| 24 | 4 | |
| 12 | 1 | |
| 24 | | 3 |
| | 2 | 12 |
| 12 | | 6 |

# Writing Equations

In each table below, the numbers in the ☐ column are dividends. The numbers in the △ column are quotients. Find the divisor that works for each table. Then, write the equation below the table, and complete the table. The first equation has been written for you.

**1.**

| ☐ | △ |
|----|----|
| 4 | 2 |
| 8 | 4 |
| 0 | |
| 6 | 3 |
| 10 | |
| 20 | |
| | 7 |

Equation:

$$\square \div 2 = \triangle$$

**2.**

| ☐ | △ |
|----|----|
| 15 | 3 |
| 35 | 7 |
| 10 | 2 |
| 25 | |
| 5 | |
| 0 | |
| 45 | |

Equation:

_____

**3.**

| ☐ | △ |
|----|----|
| 20 | 5 |
| 16 | 4 |
| 4 | 1 |
| 12 | |
| | 2 |
| | 9 |
| | 0 |

Equation:

_____

**4.**

| ☐ | △ |
|----|----|
| 12 | 2 |
| 24 | 4 |
| 6 | 1 |
| | 5 |
| | 7 |
| 0 | |
| 18 | |

Equation:

_____

**5.**

| ☐ | △ |
|----|----|
| 12 | 4 |
| 27 | 9 |
| 6 | 2 |
| | 1 |
| | 0 |
| 18 | |
| 9 | |

Equation:

_____

**6.**

| ☐ | △ |
|----|----|
| 4 | 4 |
| 8 | 8 |
| 7 | 7 |
| 5 | |
| 0 | |
| 3 | |
| 2 | |

Equation:

_____

# Follow the Arrows

Follow the arrows to solve each problem. Write
the answer inside the answer box. You may use a
multiplication table to help you multiply and divide.

1. $\boxed{27}$ → $\boxed{\div 3}$ → $\boxed{\times 2}$ → $\boxed{\div 6}$ → $\boxed{\phantom{00}}$

2. $\boxed{45}$ → $\boxed{\div 9}$ → $\boxed{+ 5}$ → $\boxed{\div 2}$ → $\boxed{\phantom{00}}$

3. $\boxed{24}$ → $\boxed{\div 4}$ → $\boxed{\times 3}$ → $\boxed{- 3}$ → $\boxed{\phantom{00}}$

4. $\boxed{3}$ → $\boxed{\times 8}$ → $\boxed{\div 6}$ → $\boxed{- 4}$ → $\boxed{\phantom{00}}$

5. $\boxed{5}$ → $\boxed{\times 5}$ → $\boxed{+ 5}$ → $\boxed{\div 5}$ → $\boxed{\phantom{00}}$

Write an operation and a number in the empty box.

6. $\boxed{48}$ → $\boxed{\div 6}$ → $\boxed{\div 2}$ → $\boxed{\phantom{00}}$ → $\boxed{16}$

7. $\boxed{36}$ → $\boxed{\div 9}$ → $\boxed{\times 2}$ → $\boxed{\phantom{00}}$ → $\boxed{2}$

8. $\boxed{4}$ → $\boxed{\times 7}$ → $\boxed{+ 4}$ → $\boxed{\phantom{00}}$ → $\boxed{8}$

Make up your own Follow the Arrows problems. Use at
least one multiplication or division step in each.

9. $\boxed{\phantom{00}}$ → $\boxed{\phantom{00}}$ → $\boxed{\phantom{00}}$ → $\boxed{\phantom{00}}$ → $\boxed{\phantom{00}}$

10. $\boxed{\phantom{00}}$ → $\boxed{\phantom{00}}$ → $\boxed{\phantom{00}}$ → $\boxed{\phantom{00}}$ → $\boxed{\phantom{00}}$

11. $\boxed{\phantom{00}}$ → $\boxed{\phantom{00}}$ → $\boxed{\phantom{00}}$ → $\boxed{\phantom{00}}$ → $\boxed{\phantom{00}}$

# The Dividing Path

Play with a partner.

**Materials:** 2 game tokens
4 sets of number cards with the
numbers 7, 8, and 9

**How to Play:**

Place the game tokens on Start. Turn the number cards upside down, or place them in a bag.

Take turns drawing a number card. Move to the closest space with a quotient that matches the number on the card. Write the quotient in the space. The first player to reach Finish wins!

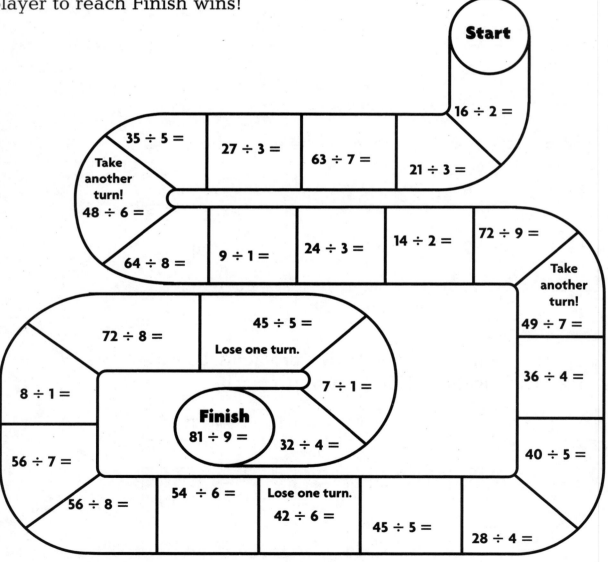

# Table Talk

Complete the table and solve each problem.

1. Mr. Brown uses 1 can of food to feed 3 cats. How many cans of food does Mr. Brown need to feed 12 cats?

| Cans | 1 | | | |
|------|---|---|---|---|
| Cats | 3 | | | |

_____

2. In Jill's class, 1 out of every 5 students walks to school. There are 25 students in the class. How many students walk to school?

| Walkers | 1 | | | | |
|---------|---|---|---|---|---|
| Students | 5 | | | | |

_____

3. During the summer, Liza reads about 2 books every 5 days. If she keeps reading at this rate, about how many books will she read in 30 days?

| Books | 2 | | | | |
|-------|---|---|---|---|---|
| Days | 5 | | | | |

_____

4. Last summer, it rained 2 days out of every 7. If it rains at the same rate this summer, how many days of rain will there be during 35 days?

| Rainy days | 2 | | | | |
|------------|---|---|---|---|---|
| Days | 7 | | | | |

_____

5. In Tom's class, 2 out of 3 students buy the school lunch. There are 21 students in the class. How many students buy the school lunch?

| Students who buy lunch | 2 | | | | | |
|------------------------|---|---|---|---|---|---|
| Students | 3 | | | | | |

_____

# Solving Problems at the Aquarium

| Aquarium | Admission | Sea Lion Show |
|---|---|---|
| | $6 adults<br>$4 children under 12<br>$45 Family membership—<br>free admission for one year | 10:30, 12:00, 1:30, 3:00 |

1. Mr. and Mrs. Young and their 6-year-old triplets go to the aquarium. How much do they pay?

_____

2. The sea lion show lasts 45 minutes. How much time is there between shows?

_____

3. The theater where the sea lions perform can seat 600 people. There are 475 people sitting in the theater for the 12:00 show. How many more people can be seated before the theater is full?

_____

4. Mr. Ruiz buys a family membership. He goes to the aquarium with his 4-year-old son 6 times during the year. How much money does he save?

_____

5. A class of 24 students visits the aquarium. They divide into 4 groups. How many students are in each group?

_____

6. John buys a book about sharks for $4.95 and a shell for $1.35. How much money does he spend?

_____

7. Meg counts 12 starfish and 9 hermit crabs in a display. How many more starfish are there than hermit crabs?

_____

8. Jesse learned that a seahorse egg hatches in 50 to 60 days. About how many weeks is this?

_____

# Un-Organized

Sam collects dolls from around the world. The table
shows what kinds of dolls he has in his collection.

| SAM'S DOLLS | | | |
|---|---|---|---|
| **Number** | **Country** | **Gender** | **Adult or Child** |
| 2 | Australia | Male | Adult |
| 3 | Australia | Female | Adult |
| 1 | Australia | Female | Child |
| 4 | Australia | Female | Child |
| 1 | United States | Female | Adult |
| 4 | United States | Male | Child |
| 5 | United States | Female | Child |
| 1 | Sweden | Male | Adult |
| 2 | Japan | Male | Adult |
| 3 | Japan | Female | Adult |
| 4 | Japan | Male | Child |
| 5 | Mexico | Female | Child |
| 3 | Israel | Male | Adult |
| 2 | Israel | Female | Child |

He sorted his dolls into four boxes. Each doll in the box
has something in common. Write what type of doll is in
each box.

_____

# Reading and Math

Which letter in the alphabet is used the most often and which is used the least often? Read a page in a book and record how often each letter is used.

| Letter | Tallies | Letter | Tallies |
|:------:|---------|:------:|---------|
| A |  | N |  |
| B |  | O |  |
| C |  | P |  |
| D |  | Q |  |
| E |  | R |  |
| F |  | S |  |
| G |  | T |  |
| H |  | U |  |
| I |  | V |  |
| J |  | W |  |
| K |  | X |  |
| L |  | Y |  |
| M |  | Z |  |

Which letter is used most often? Least often?

_____

_____

# Spinning

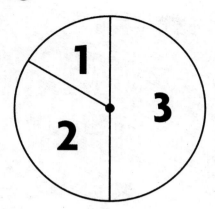

Use a paper clip and a pencil.

Put your pencil in the paper clip to hold the paper clip in the center point of the circle.

Spin the paper clip on each spinner.

Record the sum of the two numbers you spin in the table.

Repeat this 50 times.

1. Which sum happened the most?

   _____

   _____

   _____

2. Which sum happened the least?

   _____

   _____

| SPINNER EXPERIMENT | |
| --- | --- |
| Sum | Tallies |
| 5 | |
| 6 | |
| 7 | |
| 8 | |
| 9 | |

3. Why do you think the sums 7 and 8 happened more times?

   _____

   _____

# You Decide

You work at a grocery store.

You must decide what brand of chips to order.

A survey is conducted to help you.

Think about the price of the chips and the number of votes when you decide.

| CHIPS | | |
|---|---|---|
| **Brand of Chips** | **Number of Votes** | **Price per Bag** |
| Wavy | 23 | 30¢ |
| Light 'n' Salty | 13 | 36¢ |
| Crispy Crunchies | 45 | 27¢ |
| Toasties | 22 | 20¢ |
| Frickles | 61 | 23¢ |
| Ring-a-Ling | 48 | 18¢ |
| Goodies | 27 | 25¢ |

Examine the table. Pick three brands to order.
Explain your decision.

_____

_____

_____

_____

_____

# You Group

The first table shows one way to group the shapes below.
Find another way to group the shapes. Then make a table
to show the other way.

| NUMBER OF LINES | | | |
|---|---|---|---|
| | **One Line** | **Two Lines** | **Four Lines** |
| Circles | | | |
| Triangles | | | |

| | | | | |
|---|---|---|---|---|
| | | | | |
| | | | | |
| | | | | |

# Symbols of Saving

Henry is saving his money. He has made a pictograph
of how much he has saved each week.

| Saving Money | |
|---|---|
| First Week | 🪙 🪙 |
| Second Week | 🪙 🪙 🪙 🪙 🪙 |
| Third Week | 🪙 🪙 🪙 🪙 🪙 🪙 🪙 🪙 |
| Fourth Week | 🪙 🪙 🪙 🪙 🪙 🪙 🪙 🪙 🪙 🪙 🪙 |
| Fifth Week | 🪙 🪙 🪙 🪙 🪙 🪙 🪙 🪙 🪙 🪙 🪙 🪙 🪙 🪙 |
| Sixth Week | 🪙 🪙 🪙 🪙 🪙 🪙 🪙 🪙 🪙 🪙 🪙 🪙 🪙 🪙 🪙 🪙 🪙 |
| Seventh Week | 🪙 🪙 🪙 🪙 🪙 🪙 🪙 🪙 🪙 🪙 🪙 🪙 🪙 🪙 🪙 🪙 🪙 🪙 🪙 🪙 |

Key: Each 🪙 stands for 5 pennies.

1. How much money did he save each week?

   _____

   _____

   _____

2. If the pattern continues, how many penny symbols
   will he draw for the eighth week? for the ninth week?

   _____

3. Complete the table for the eighth through the tenth weeks.

| | |
|---|---|
| Eighth Week | |
| Ninth Week | |
| Tenth Week | |

4. Henry wants to buy a new kite. The kite costs $2.25.
   During what week will Henry save enough for the
   new kite?

   _____

# Parts of a Picture

The pictograph shows the number of students in
seven third-grade classes.

| Third-Grade Classes | |
|---|---|
| Mr. Jones | 大大大大大大大 |
| Mrs. Smith | 大大大大大大𝟣 |
| Mr. Tilling | 大大大大大大大 |
| Mr. Brown | 大大大大大大大大𝟣 |
| Ms. Triggs | 大大大大大大 |
| Mrs. Hanson | 大大大大大大大𝟣 |
| Mrs. Wright | 大大大大大大𝟣 |

Key: Each 大 stands for 4 students.

1. Each 大 stands for how many students?

_____

2. Each 𝟣 stands for how many students? Explain.

_____

_____

3. Each 𝟣 stands for how many students? Explain.

_____

_____

4. List how many students each teacher has in order
   from most students to fewest students.

_____

_____

# What Is Left?

Starting with 2, put a diagonal line from upper left to lower right through every second number.

Starting with 3, put a diagonal line from lower left to upper right through every third number.

Starting with 5, put a vertical line through every fifth number.

Starting with 7, put a horizontal line through every seventh number.

| 1 | 2 | 3 | 4 | 5 | 6 | 7 | 8 | 9 | 10 |
|---|---|---|---|---|---|---|---|---|---|
| 11 | 12 | 13 | 14 | 15 | 16 | 17 | 18 | 19 | 20 |
| 21 | 22 | 23 | 24 | 25 | 26 | 27 | 28 | 29 | 30 |
| 31 | 32 | 33 | 34 | 35 | 36 | 37 | 38 | 39 | 40 |
| 41 | 42 | 43 | 44 | 45 | 46 | 47 | 48 | 49 | 50 |
| 51 | 52 | 53 | 54 | 55 | 56 | 57 | 58 | 59 | 60 |
| 61 | 62 | 63 | 64 | 65 | 66 | 67 | 68 | 69 | 70 |
| 71 | 72 | 73 | 74 | 75 | 76 | 77 | 78 | 79 | 80 |
| 81 | 82 | 83 | 84 | 85 | 86 | 87 | 88 | 89 | 90 |
| 91 | 92 | 93 | 94 | 95 | 96 | 97 | 98 | 99 | 100 |

1. Circle any numbers not marked. What numbers are circled?

_____

_____

2. Which numbers have all four types of lines drawn through them?

_____

# Pay Up

Mr. Santos rewards his students for doing their homework. Each time they do a homework assignment he gives them a smiling face sticker. When students have collected 8 smiling face stickers, they receive a pencil.

Complete the chart for each student.

| Name | Stickers | Number of Pencils | Stickers Left Over |
|------|----------|-------------------|--------------------|
| Sylvia | ☺☺☺☺☺☺☺ | | |
| Joshua | ☺☺☺☺☺☺☺☺☺☺☺☺☺☺☺ | | |
| Kendra | ☺☺☺☺☺☺☺☺☺☺☺☺ ☺☺☺☺☺☺☺☺☺☺☺☺ | | |
| Brandon | ☺☺☺☺☺☺☺☺☺☺☺ ☺☺☺☺☺ | | |
| Jessica | ☺☺☺☺☺☺☺☺☺☺☺☺ | | |
| Martha | ☺☺☺☺☺☺☺☺☺☺☺☺☺ ☺☺☺☺☺☺☺☺☺☺☺☺☺ | | |
| Tiffany | ☺☺☺☺☺☺☺☺☺☺☺ | | |
| Stacey | ☺☺☺ | | |
| Tony | ☺☺☺☺☺☺☺☺☺☺☺ ☺☺☺☺☺☺☺☺☺☺☺ | | |
| Justin | ☺☺☺☺☺☺☺☺☺☺☺☺☺☺☺ | | |
| Paola | ☺☺☺☺☺☺☺☺☺☺☺☺ ☺☺☺☺☺☺☺☺☺☺☺☺ ☺☺☺☺☺☺☺☺☺☺☺☺ | | |

1. Who got the most pencils? the fewest pencils?

_____

2. If they all decided to share, are there enough pencils? Explain.

_____

# The Riddle

What did the little tree say when
it was all grown up?

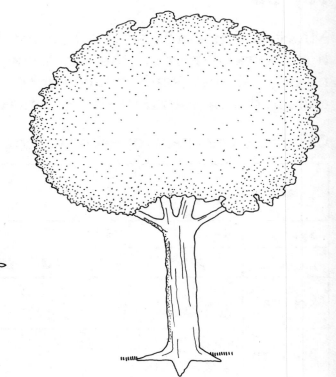

To find out, solve each problem. Put the letter for each
problem above the answer at the bottom of the page.

|              I               |              T               |              E               |
|------------------------------|------------------------------|------------------------------|
| **1.** $7 \times 2 =$ _____  | **2.** $2 + 2 + 1 + 1 =$ _____ | **3.** $5 \times 3 + 2 =$ _____ |

|              E               |             'M               |              G               |
|------------------------------|------------------------------|------------------------------|
| **4.** $17 - 2 =$ _____      | **5.** $7 + 7 + 7 + 7 =$ _____ | **6.** $5 \times 2 + 1 + 1 =$ _____ |

|              E               |              R               |              E               |
|------------------------------|------------------------------|------------------------------|
| **7.** $6 \times 4 - 1 =$ _____ | **8.** $3 \times 3 + 1 =$ _____ | **9.** $5 \times 3 - 4 =$ _____ |

A

**10.** $2 \times 2 =$ _____

$$\overline{\phantom{0}}\ \overline{\phantom{0}}\ \overline{\phantom{0}}\ \overset{\textstyle '}{}\ \overline{\phantom{0}}\ \overline{\phantom{0}}\ \overline{\phantom{0}}\ \overline{\phantom{0}}\ \overline{\phantom{0}}\ \overline{\phantom{0}}$$
12   15   23      14   28      4      6   10   17   11

# The Survey Says!

Ask 34 students at school in which month they were born. Record your data in the tally table at the right and fill in the survey.

| Birthdays | |
|-----------|--------|
| **Month** | **Tallies** |
| January | |
| February | |
| March | |
| April | |
| May | |
| June | |
| July | |
| August | |
| September | |
| October | |
| November | |
| December | |

Complete the vertical bar graph using the data from your survey.

**Number of Birthdays**

1. What month had the most students? the fewest students?

_____

2. Did you find two people with the same birthday?

_____

_____

# Chip Away

## Game Board

| | | | | | | |
|---|---|---|---|---|---|---|
| 3 | 5 | 2 | 5 | 3 | 3 | 1 |
| 4 | 3 | 2 | 3 | 5 | 2 | 5 |
| 4 | 5 | 6 | 1 | 3 | 3 | 1 |
| 3 | 2 | 4 | 2 | 5 | 4 | 2 |

Emily and Susan take turns dropping a counter on the game board. All squares have the same chance of being landed on. Answer each question.

**1.** What is the most likely outcome on the game board? Why?

_____

_____

**2.** What is the least likely outcome? Why?

_____

_____

**3.** Shade in the numbers that have the same chance of being landed on. What are those numbers?

_____

**4.** Which is more likely, landing on a 1 or a 4? Why?

_____

_____

# Spinner Fun

Use a paperclip and a pencil to make a spinner. Spin it 12 times. Record the results in the table with tally marks.

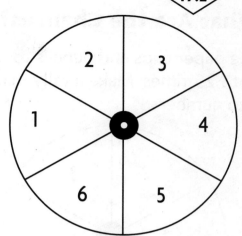

| Number | 1 | 2 | 3 | 4 | 5 | 6 | 7 | 8 | 9 | 10 | 11 | 12 |
|--------|---|---|---|---|---|---|---|---|---|----|----|----|
| Times Spun | | | | | | | | | | | | |

Repeat the activity. Record the results.

| Number | 1 | 2 | 3 | 4 | 5 | 6 | 7 | 8 | 9 | 10 | 11 | 12 |
|--------|---|---|---|---|---|---|---|---|---|----|----|----|
| Times Spun | | | | | | | | | | | | |

Answer the questions.

1. Did you spin any number more often the second time than the first time?

   _____

2. Did you spin any number fewer times?

   _____

3. Did you spin any numbers the same number of times?

   _____

4. If the results are different, write why you think so.

   _____

   _____

5. Graph the results of your experiments.

   _____

   _____

   _____

# What Are the Chances?

Use paper clips and pencils to make two spinners. Spin them both 25 times. Make a tally mark to record the sum of the two numbers.

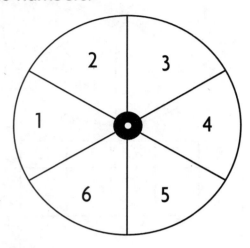 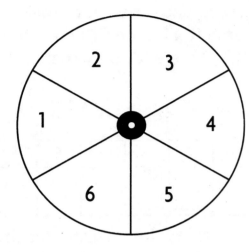

| Sum | 2 | 3 | 4 | 5 | 6 | 7 | 8 | 9 | 10 | 11 | 12 |
|-----|---|---|---|---|---|---|---|---|----|----|----|
| Tally | | | | | | | | | | | |

Use your tally marks to answer the questions.

1. What is the lowest possible sum you can spin? the greatest?

   _____

2. Which sum did you spin most often?

   _____

3. Which sums were not spun at all or spun least often?

   _____

4. Were the sums near the middle of the tally spun more often than those near the edges?

   _____

5. Why do you think that is so?

   _____

# Nature Hunt

Mrs. Brown's third-grade class is going on a nature hunt.
The class is arranged in four groups. Each group has been
given a list of items to find. They have ten minutes to find
what is on the list. Look at the pictures, and then answer
the following questions.

1. Is it likely or unlikely that
   one group won't find any
   of the items?

   _____

   _____

   _____

   _____

2. If one group has only two
   people, what is the most
   likely outcome of their hunt?

   _____

   _____

   _____

3. Mrs. Brown told the four
   groups each to make up a
   name that relates to nature.
   What are some possible
   names for groups?

   _____

   _____

4. If Mrs. Brown teaches in
   Minnesota, in which season is
   she least likely to take her
   class out on a nature hunt?

   _____

# Star Power!

With which spinner would you have a better chance
of getting the outcome? Write *Spinner 1* or *Spinner 2*.
Explain your choice.

**Spinner 1**   **Spinner 2**

1. stopping on an odd number

   _____

   _____

   _____

2. stopping on the product of 8
   and 9

   _____

   _____

   _____

3. stopping on a number with
   digits that add up to 6

   _____

   _____

   _____

4. stopping on a number with a
   1 in the tens place

   _____

   _____

   _____

5. stopping on a number that is
   greater than 50

   _____

   _____

6. stopping on a number that is
   less than 60

   _____

   _____

# The Solid Figure Path

Play with a partner.

**Materials:** one number cube, a game token for each player

**How to Play:**

- Place the game tokens on Start. Roll the number cube and move that many spaces.

- If you land on a space with the name of a solid figure, name an object that has that shape. If you are incorrect, go back two spaces.

- If you land on a space with a question, answer the question. If you are incorrect, go back two spaces.

- The first player to reach Finish is the winner.

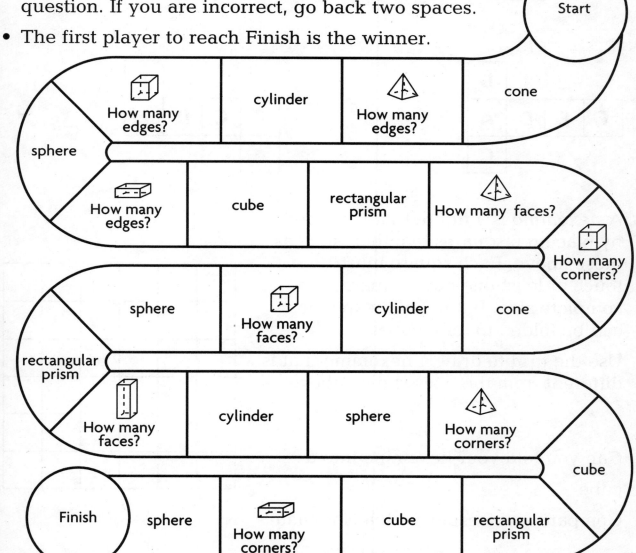

# Folding Cubes

When each figure is folded to form a cube, what letter
will be on the side opposite the side marked **A**?

You may trace, cut, and fold the figures to check your answers.

1. _____

```
        A
B | C | D | E
        F
```

2. _____

```
            E
A | B | C | D
        F
```

3. _____

```
            B
F | E | D | A
            C
```

4. _____

```
                F
B | C | D | E
A
```

5. A *hexomino* is a figure that is formed
by placing 6 squares together, such as
those above. Each square must
touch at least one other square on a
complete side, but not all hexominos
can be folded to form cubes.

Use the grid to draw a hexomino that is
different from the ones shown above.

Can you fold your hexomino into a

cube? _____

Compare your results with a classmate's.

# New Faces

Suppose you cut each of these solid figures into two parts
that look the same. What would be the shape of
the faces formed by the cuts?

1.     2.     3.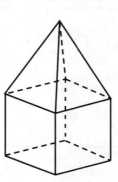

_____     _____     _____

4. Simon glued two identical square
   pyramids together at the squares.

   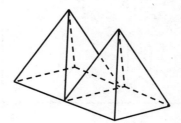

   • How many faces does the new

     solid figure have? _____

   • How many edges? _____

5. Naomi glued one cube next to another
   that is the same size.

   • How many faces does the new

     solid figure have? _____

   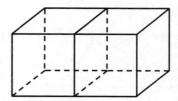

   • How many edges? _____

   • How many corners? _____

6. Peter glued a square pyramid on top
   of a cube. The square face of the pyramid
   is the same size as each face of the cube.

   • How many faces does the new

     solid figure have? _____

   • How many edges? _____

   • How many corners? _____

# Figure Families

The groups of figures in the left-hand boxes below are different
from the groups in the center boxes. Draw a new figure in
the right-hand boxes that could be a member of the group
in the left-hand boxes. Then describe how they are alike.

**1.**

| These are Flobs. | These are *not* Flobs. | Draw a Flob. |
|---|---|---|
| | | |

Flobs are _____.

**2.**

| These are Trogs. | These are *not* Trogs. | Draw a Trog. |
|---|---|---|
| | | |

Trogs are _____.

**3.**

| These are Bligs. | These are *not* Bligs. | Draw a Blig. |
|---|---|---|
| | | |

Bligs are _____.

# Patterns with Dots

Circle the part of the pattern that repeats. Then continue each pattern.

**1.**

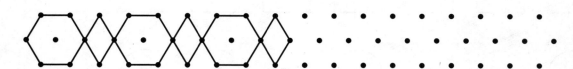

**2.**

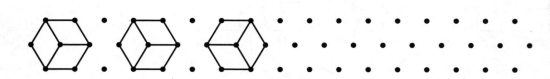

**3.**

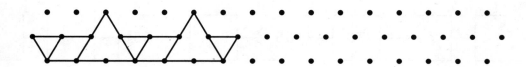

**4.**

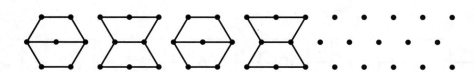

**5.**

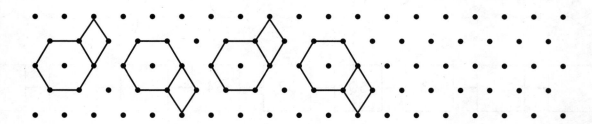

# Number Patterns

Find each pattern. Fill in the missing numbers or letters.

1. | 3 | 6 | 9 | 12 | | | | | |

2. A — B — C — B — C — D — C — ◯ — ◯

3. | | 22 | | 44 | 55 | | | | |

4. 1 — 10 — 2 — 9 — 3 — ◯ — ◯ — ◯ — ◯ — ◯

5. | | | 75 | 70 | 65 | | 55 | | |

6. 1 — A — A — 2 — ◯ — B — 3 — C — ◯ — ◯ — ◯ — D — ◯ — ◯ — ◯

7. | | 202 | | | 505 | 606 | | | |

8. A — B — A — C — ◯ — D — A — ◯ — ◯ — ◯ — A

9. | | | 43 | 50 | 57 | 64 | | | |

# Get in Line

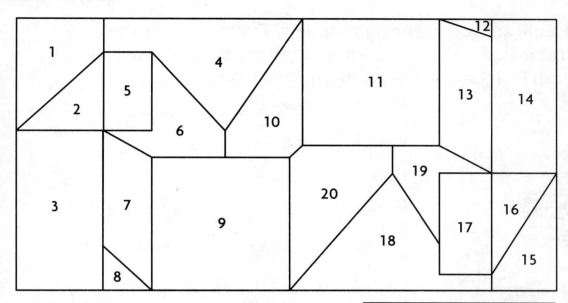

Answer the following questions and then follow the directions.

1. What numbered shapes have four line segments?

_____

2. What numbered shapes have three line segments?

_____

3. What numbered shapes have five or more line segments?

_____

4. Use the chart to color the figures.

5. Make your own design using figures with line segments. Color the design.

| Numbers | Color |
|---------|-------|
| 1,15 | Black |
| 2,16 | Red |
| 3,14 | Yellow |
| 7,13 | Green |
| 8,12 | Orange |
| 5,17 | Purple |
| 6,19 | Brown |
| 10,20 | Blue |
| 9,11 | Pink |
| 4,18 | Light Blue |

# Grocery List

Raul and Laurie are going grocery shopping. They have split the shopping list in half. Below is a map of the store showing where the items can be found. Tell what items Raul and Laurie buy.

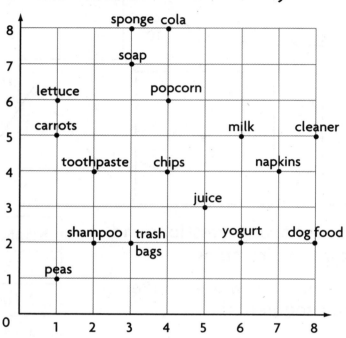

| **Laurie's list** | | **Raul's list** |
|---|---|---|

**1.** (1,1) _____ (4,4) _____

**2.** (3,7) _____ (2,2) _____

**3.** (8,2) _____ (7,4) _____

**4.** (5,3) _____ (6,5) _____

**5.** (3,2) _____ (1,5) _____

**6.** (8,5) _____ (4,8) _____

**7.** (6,2) _____ (3,8) _____

**8.** (1,6) _____ (4,6) _____

**9.** If Raul and Laurie go to (2,4), where do they meet?

_____

# Congruent Figure Detective

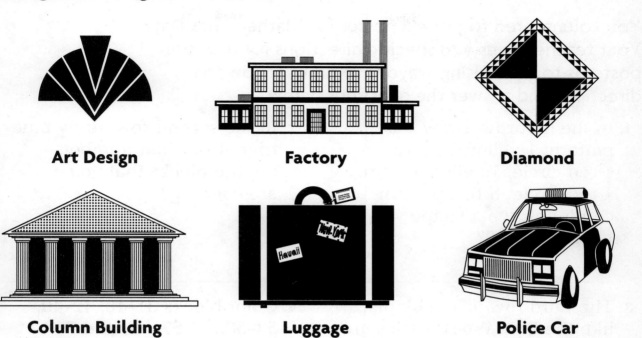

**Art Design**

**Factory**

**Diamond**

**Column Building**

**Luggage**

**Police Car**

List the congruent figures you see on the pictures.

| Picture | Shapes |
|---------|--------|
|         |        |
|         |        |
|         |        |
|         |        |
|         |        |
|         |        |

# Poster Maker

You volunteered to make a poster for Mathematics Day.
Your teacher gives you specific directions for how the
poster is to look. Using crayons to draw, follow the
directions and answer the questions below.

1. In the first row, draw this
   pattern: 1 yellow square,
   1 red circle, 1 yellow square,
   1 red circle. If this pattern
   continues, what shape will
   be in block 10?

   _____

2. In the second row, draw blue
   triangles. What numbers
   are the blocks that you
   are coloring?

   _____

3. The third row is to look just
   like the first. What shapes are
   you drawing in the third row?

   _____

4. Color blocks 31–40, 42–49,
   53–58, 64–67, 75, and 76
   orange. About how many
   blocks in all did you color
   orange?

   _____

5. Color half of the blocks
   41, 50, 52, 59, 63, 68, 74,
   77, 85, and 86 orange.
   What shape did you just
   complete?

   _____

6. For the remaining
   blocks, pick the final
   color. What shapes does
   the final color make?

   _____

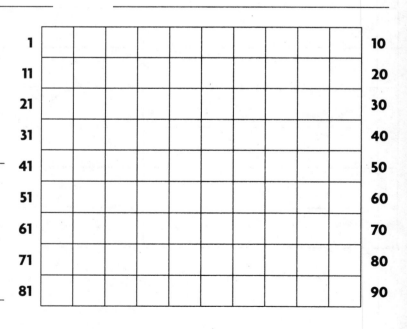

# Out the Door!

Freddie needs to find his way out of the building. Can you help him get to the bottom floor and out the door? Find the answers to the exercises below. If the answer appears on the building, color in that numbered block. When you finish, you will see Freddie's path out of the building.

| 45 | 36 | 27 | 21 | 0 |
|----|----|----|----|----|
| 18 | 16 | 15 | 14 | 6 |
| 49 | 33 | 5 | 3 | 8 |
| 19 | 54 | 7 | 2 | 11 |
| 10 | 25 | 9 | 4 | 20 |

**1.** $12 \div 4 =$ _____

**2.** $3 \times 5 =$ _____

**3.** $16 \div 4 =$ _____

**4.** $2 \times 8 =$ _____

**5.** $28 \div 4 =$ _____

**6.** $36 \div 4 =$ _____

**7.** $3 \times 7 =$ _____

**8.** $2 \times 6 =$ _____

**9.** $30 \div 6 =$ _____

**10.** $9 \times 5 =$ _____

**11.** $2 \times 7 =$ _____

**12.** $6 \times 3 =$ _____

**13.** $24 \div 3 =$ _____

**14.** $6 \times 6 =$ _____

**15.** $10 \div 2 =$ _____

**16.** $8 \times 4 =$ _____

**17.** $4 \times 5 =$ _____

**18.** $1 \times 0 =$ _____

# What Do You See?

Look carefully at the pictures below. Decide whether the pictures are the same or different. Then answer the questions, naming what each picture has. Be careful, though—things aren't always what they appear to be!

**Picture 1**

**Picture 2**

1. What do the pictures have in common?

_____

_____

_____

2. Are the pictures congruent? Explain.

_____

_____

_____

3. Do you see anything that is different in the pictures?

_____

_____

_____

_____

4. How can you make the pictures more alike?

_____

_____

_____

_____

# Design a Pattern

You have been asked to design a new type of gift wrap.
Your design must include 3 shapes, such as 3 letters,
3 numbers, 3 math signs, or 3 punctuation marks. Your
design must include examples of each shape in flips,
slides, and turns.

Sketch your design in the space. Use crayons or markers
to color your design.

# Moving by Slides, Flips, and Turns

Follow the directions and the figures to keep each pattern going.

**1.** Keep on flipping...

 _____

**2.** Turn, turn back, and flip...

 _____

**3.** Flip and slide...

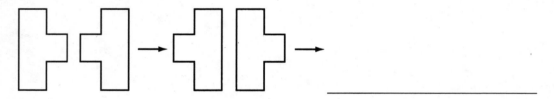 _____

**4.** Slide, flip, and flip...

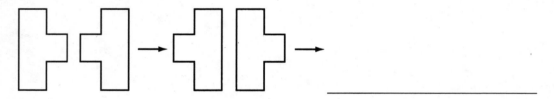 _____

**5.** Turn, slide, and flip...

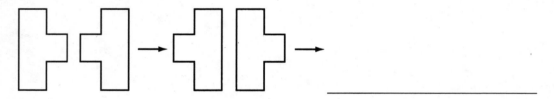 _____

# Lines of Symmetry Around You

You can make drawings of common household objects and natural objects—drawings that have one or more lines of symmetry.

With a partner or with your whole class, see how many objects you can draw that have lines of symmetry. Set a timer and draw for 15 minutes. Then score a point for each line of symmetry that can be drawn on your objects. Whoever scores the most points wins!

# Blooms and Balloons

Complete the drawings below to show what you would
see if you held the half drawings up to a mirror.

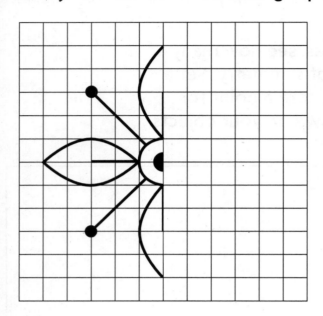

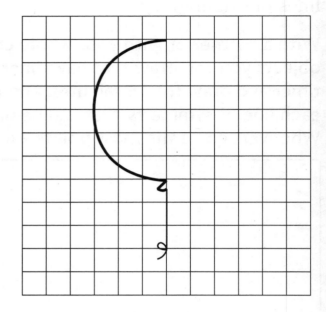

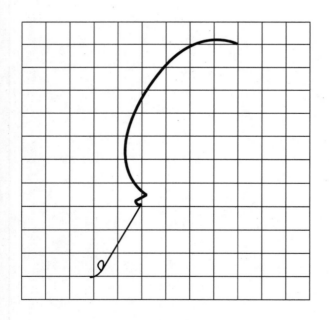

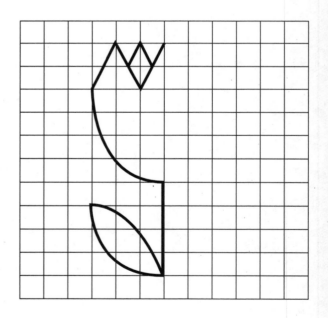

# Symmetry Street

Ava Tut lives at 181 Symmetry Street. The buildings
on each side of the street mirror those on the other.
Also, each building can be divided by its own line of
symmetry. Everyone who lives on Symmetry Street
has a name and street number that can be divided by
a line of symmetry.

Draw the other side of Symmetry Street, and decorate the
buildings on both sides of the street so they are symmetric.
Write a family name and address for the other house on
the street.

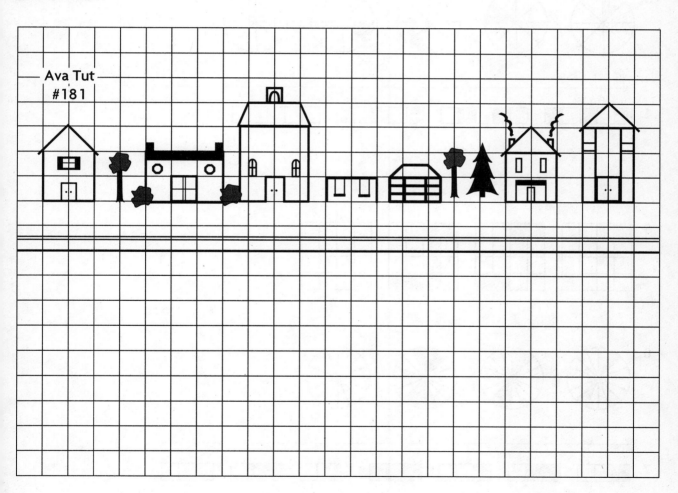

# Parts 'n' Patterns

Shade the last, unshaded shape in a way to continue the
pattern the first shapes start. Tell how many parts make up
the last shape. Then tell how many parts you have shaded.

1.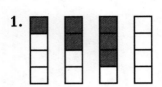

2.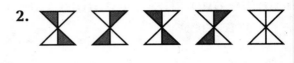

_____    _____

3.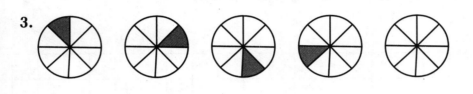

_____

4.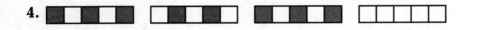

_____

5.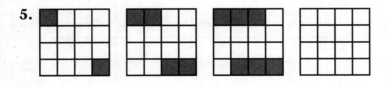

_____

6.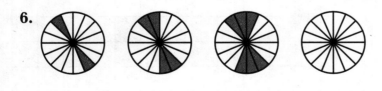

_____

7.

_____

# Fetching Fractions

Find the word name for each Column 1 fraction in
Column 2. Then write the word name's circled letter on
the line in front of the fraction.

Column 1

_____ 1. $\frac{1}{2}$

_____ 2. $\frac{3}{4}$

_____ 3. $\frac{2}{5}$

_____ 4. $\frac{1}{3}$

_____ 5. $\frac{6}{7}$

_____ 6. $\frac{2}{9}$

_____ 7. $\frac{4}{7}$

_____ 8. $\frac{5}{9}$

_____ 9. $\frac{4}{15}$

_____ 10. $\frac{1}{10}$

_____ 11. $\frac{9}{11}$

_____ 12. $\frac{1}{5}$

_____ 13. $\frac{7}{8}$

_____ 14. $\frac{8}{9}$

Column 2

(A) two fifths

(C) two ninths

(E) five divided by nine

(F) four out of seven

(H) one tenth

(I) seven divided by eight

(L) one out of two

(N) four fifteenths

(O) six sevenths

(P) one out of five

(R) eight ninths

(S) three divided by four

(T) nine elevenths

(W) one out of three

Now decode the sentence below. The numbers tell you where to look
in Column 1. Write the letter that is on the blank in front of the fraction.

___ ___ ___ ___ ___ ___ ___ ___ ___ ___ ___
 3    7   14   3    6   11   13   5    9   13   2

___ ___ ___ ___ ___ ___ ___ ___ ___ ___ ___ ___ .
12   3   14   11   5    7    3    4   10   5    1    8

# Model the Whole

Create a model that fits each description. Draw your
model in the space. Then answer the questions about
each model.

1. A square with
   - 8 equal parts
   - 3 parts shaded

   a. What fractional part of the
      model is shaded? _____

   b. How many fractional parts
      make up the model? _____

2. A circle with
   - 4 equal parts
   - 3 parts shaded

   a. What fractional part of the
      model is shaded? _____

   b. How many fractional parts
      make up the model? _____

3. A rectangle with
   - 10 equal parts
   - 7 parts striped
   - 2 parts polka dotted

   a. What fractional part of the
      model is striped? _____

   b. What fractional part of the
      model is striped or polka

      dotted? _____

   c. How many fractional parts

      make up the model? _____

4. A hexagon with
   - 6 equal parts
   - 3 parts filled with stars
   - 1 part filled with diamonds

   a. What fractional part of the
      model is not decorated? ____

   b. What fractional part of the

      model is decorated? _____

   c. How many fractional parts

      make up the model? _____

# Fraction Action

Follow the directions to make a new fraction. Then draw both fractions in the fraction bars by dividing each bar into the correct number of parts and shading the parts used. Finally, compare the fractions and mark <, >, or = in the center ◯.

1. $\frac{3}{4}$ $\longrightarrow$ same numerator;
add 2 to the denominator $\longrightarrow$

2. $\frac{4}{6}$ $\longrightarrow$ add 2 to the numerator;
add 2 to the denominator $\longrightarrow$

3. $\frac{5}{8}$ $\longrightarrow$ add 1 to the numerator;
same denominator $\longrightarrow$

4. $\frac{2}{3}$ $\longrightarrow$ add 2 to the numerator;
add 3 to the denominator $\longrightarrow$

5. $\frac{3}{8}$ $\longrightarrow$ same numerator;
subtract 4 from the denominator $\longrightarrow$

6. $\frac{2}{12}$ $\longrightarrow$ add 5 to the numerator;
same denominator $\longrightarrow$

7. $\frac{3}{5}$ $\longrightarrow$ add 1 to the numerator;
subtract 1 from the denominator $\longrightarrow$

# Fraction Patterns

Look at the bottom of the page for the missing fraction or whole number in each fraction pattern below. Write on the line above the missing fraction or whole number the circled letter that is next to the fraction pattern. (Some letters appear more than once.)

1. $\frac{5}{16}$, $\frac{4}{16}$, _____, $\frac{2}{16}$   (R)

2. $\frac{1}{2}$, 1, _____, 2   (T)

3. $8\frac{1}{3}$, _____, 9, $9\frac{1}{3}$   (S)

4. $9\frac{2}{5}$, _____, $9\frac{4}{5}$, 10   (A)

5. $5\frac{6}{8}$, $5\frac{7}{8}$, _____, $6\frac{1}{8}$   (O)

6. $\frac{1}{7}$, _____, $\frac{5}{7}$, 1   (I)

7. 3, $2\frac{4}{6}$, _____, 2   (C)

8. $2\frac{2}{3}$, 3, _____, $3\frac{2}{3}$   (N)

9. $\frac{9}{12}$, _____, $\frac{11}{12}$, 1   (E)

10. $12\frac{1}{2}$, 12, $11\frac{1}{2}$, _____   (F)

11. 2, _____, $1\frac{2}{6}$, 1   (L)

12. $1\frac{3}{9}$, $1\frac{5}{9}$, _____, 2   (V)

13. 10, _____, 9, $8\frac{1}{2}$   (H)

___ ___ ___ ___ ___ ___ ___ ___ ___
11   $\frac{3}{16}$   $9\frac{3}{5}$   $2\frac{2}{6}$   $1\frac{1}{2}$   $\frac{3}{7}$   6   $3\frac{1}{3}$   $8\frac{2}{3}$

___ ___ ___ ___   ___ ___   ___ ___ ___ ___ ___.
$1\frac{4}{6}$   6   $1\frac{7}{9}$   $\frac{10}{12}$   $1\frac{1}{2}$   6   $8\frac{2}{3}$   $9\frac{1}{2}$   $9\frac{3}{5}$   $\frac{3}{16}$   $\frac{10}{12}$

# Criss-Cross-Match

You can always use criss-cross-match to see if fractions are equivalent. How does it work? First, multiply the numerator of the first fraction by the denominator of the second and write the product down. Then, multiply the numerator of the second fraction by the denominator of the first and write that product down. If the products match, the fractions are equivalent.

$$\frac{3}{6} \diagdown\!\!\!\!\!\diagup \frac{4}{8}$$
(24)　(24)

These fractions are equivalent.

$$\frac{2}{4} \diagdown\!\!\!\!\!\diagup \frac{3}{8}$$
(12)　(16)

These fractions are not equivalent.

---

Use criss-cross-match to find the fractions that are equivalent to the fraction in the center box. Shade the fractions that are equivalent.

**1.**

| $\frac{9}{9}$ | $\frac{4}{20}$ | $\frac{6}{25}$ |
|---|---|---|
| $\frac{5}{10}$ | $\frac{1}{5}$ | $\frac{3}{8}$ |
| $\frac{7}{35}$ | $\frac{5}{6}$ | $\frac{2}{10}$ |

**2.**

| $\frac{2}{2}$ | $\frac{9}{13}$ | $\frac{15}{15}$ |
|---|---|---|
| $\frac{8}{11}$ | $\frac{12}{12}$ | $\frac{10}{11}$ |
| $\frac{9}{9}$ | $\frac{5}{10}$ | $\frac{3}{4}$ |

**3.**

| $\frac{4}{5}$ | $\frac{5}{10}$ | $\frac{2}{7}$ |
|---|---|---|
| $\frac{8}{11}$ | $\frac{1}{2}$ | $\frac{4}{8}$ |
| $\frac{3}{6}$ | $\frac{4}{5}$ | $\frac{2}{3}$ |

**4.**

| $\frac{7}{13}$ | $\frac{9}{12}$ | $\frac{2}{9}$ |
|---|---|---|
| $\frac{2}{7}$ | $\frac{3}{4}$ | $\frac{5}{11}$ |
| $\frac{12}{16}$ | $\frac{6}{8}$ | $\frac{4}{13}$ |

**5.**

| $\frac{9}{27}$ | $\frac{4}{40}$ | $\frac{3}{18}$ |
|---|---|---|
| $\frac{2}{12}$ | $\frac{1}{6}$ | $\frac{7}{35}$ |
| $\frac{5}{20}$ | $\frac{11}{28}$ | $\frac{4}{24}$ |

**6.**

| $\frac{6}{9}$ | $\frac{4}{5}$ | $\frac{7}{8}$ |
|---|---|---|
| $\frac{5}{6}$ | $\frac{2}{3}$ | $\frac{1}{2}$ |
| $\frac{8}{12}$ | $\frac{9}{13}$ | $\frac{4}{6}$ |

# A Pet Riddle

Circle the letters in those boxes that show
- 1 part shaded out of 2 equal parts, **or**
- 1 part shaded out of 3 equal parts.

Then solve the riddle by writing the circled letters in order on the blanks.

| 1.  I | 2. T | 3. S | 4. R |
|---|---|---|---|
| 5. U | 6. P | 7. M | 8. O |
| 9. N | 10. D | 11. A | 12. P |
| 13. E | 14. S | 15. E | 16. L |
| 17. T | 18. Y | 19. R | 20. S |

Which pets are the most musical?

_____  _____  _____  _____      _____  _____  _____

# Laundry and Leg Lesson

## What fraction of the shirts . . .

**1.** have long sleeves?

_____

**2.** have short sleeves?

_____

**3.** have numbers?

_____

**4.** have stripes?

_____

**5.** have numbers or stripes?

_____

**6.** have both numbers and short sleeves?

_____

## What fraction of the animals . . .

**7.** have exactly 4 legs?

_____

**8.** have exactly 2 legs?

_____

**9.** have 4 or more legs?

_____

**10.** have fur?

_____

**11.** can fly?

_____

**12.** can live in the water?

_____

**13.** have feathers?

_____

**14.** are insects?

_____

# Color the Apples

How could you color $\frac{3}{4}$ of the 8 apples red?

Look at the <u>denominator</u>.

It tells you to make
4 equal parts.

Divide the 8 apples into
4 equal groups.

Each group has 2 apples.

Look at the <u>numerator</u>.

It tells you to color
3 of the groups.

Color 3 of the 4 groups.

The picture shows
6 apples shaded.

So, $\frac{3}{4}$ of 8 = 6

Color the apples to show the part of the group the
fraction tells about. Solve.

1.

Color $\frac{1}{4}$ red.

$\frac{1}{4}$ of 12 = _____

2.

Color $\frac{3}{4}$ green.

$\frac{3}{4}$ of 12 = _____

3.

Color $\frac{1}{5}$ green.

$\frac{1}{5}$ of 15 = _____

4.

Color $\frac{2}{5}$ red.

$\frac{2}{5}$ of 15 = _____

# Group Projects

A class of 24 students worked in groups of 3 on a math project.

1. How many groups were there? _____

2. What fraction of the class was in each group? _____

The same class worked in groups of different sizes on other projects.

Write the missing information in the table.

| | Project | Number in Each Group | Number of Groups | Fraction of the Class in Each Group |
|---|---|---|---|---|
| 3. | Science | 4 | | |
| 4. | Cooking | 8 | | |
| 5. | Puppets | 6 | | |
| 6. | Art | 12 | | |
| 7. | Bookmaking | 2 | | |

8. One of the science groups had a packet of 12 seeds. They planted 3 seeds in each cup. How many cups did they use? What fraction of the seeds did they plant in each cup?

_____

9. One of the cooking groups baked 36 cookies. They put 9 cookies on each plate. How many plates did they use? What fraction of the cookies did they put on each plate?

_____

10. A math group made a design using 30 pattern blocks; $\frac{1}{5}$ of the pattern blocks were parallelograms. How many parallelograms were in the design?

_____

11. One group made 12 puppets to act out a story; $\frac{1}{3}$ of the puppets were stick puppets. How many stick puppets did the group make?

_____

# Matching Fractions

Draw lines to match each fraction to a picture in
Column A and a picture in Column B. The fractional
parts have been shaded in the pictures. The first one
has been done for you.

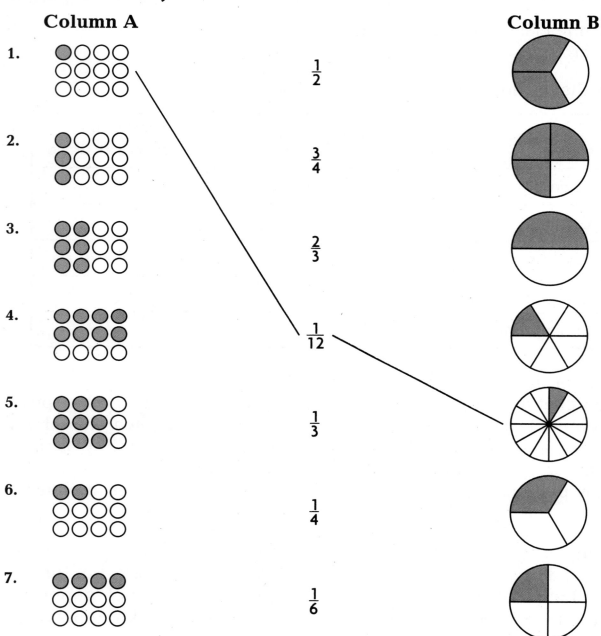

**Column A**                                                    **Column B**

1.

$\frac{1}{2}$

2.

$\frac{3}{4}$

3.

$\frac{2}{3}$

4.

$\frac{1}{12}$

5.

$\frac{1}{3}$

6.

$\frac{1}{4}$

7.

$\frac{1}{6}$

**8.** Write the fractions in order from the least to the greatest.

_____

# Parts of a Whole

Each circle or bar is divided into tenths. Use different colored crayons or pencils to show two decimal numbers that equal one whole. Then complete the equation below the picture to show how you have made one whole. The first one has been done for you.

1.

2.

3.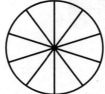

__0.3__ + __0.7__ = 1      _____ + _____ = 1      _____ + _____ = 1

4.

5.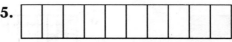

_____ + _____ = 1      _____ + _____ = 1

For each circle or bar below, use different colored crayons or pencils to show three decimal numbers that equal one whole. Then complete the equation to show how you have made one whole.

6.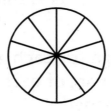

7. 

_____ + _____ + _____ = 1      _____ + _____ + _____ = 1

For each circle or bar below, use different colored crayons or pencils to show four decimal numbers that equal one whole. Then complete the equation to show how you have made one whole.

8.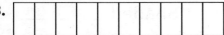

9.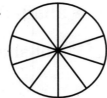

_____ + _____ + _____ + _____ = 1      _____ + _____ + _____ + _____ = 1

**STRETCH YOUR THINKING   E129**

# Decimal Designs

Write a decimal to show what part of each grid is shaded
and what part is not shaded.

**1.**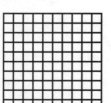

Shaded: _____

Not shaded: _____

**2.**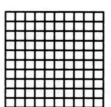

Shaded: _____

Not shaded: _____

**3.**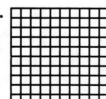

Shaded: _____

Not shaded: _____

**4.**

Shaded: _____

Not shaded: _____

**5.**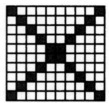

Shaded: _____

Not shaded: _____

**6.**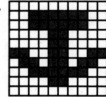

Shaded: _____

Not shaded: _____

Draw and shade a design for each grid. Then write a
decimal to show what part of each grid is shaded
and what part is not shaded.

**7.**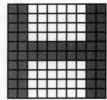

Shaded: _____

Not shaded: _____

**8.**

Shaded: _____

Not shaded: _____

**9.**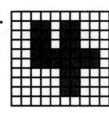

Shaded: _____

Not shaded: _____

# More Decimal Designs

Write a fraction and a decimal for each shaded part of the grid.

| | Fraction | Decimal |
|---|---|---|

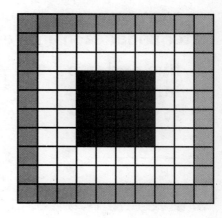

1. ■ _____ _____

2. ■ _____ _____

3. ☐ _____ _____

For Problems 4–6, use a decimal.

4. What part of the design is not white? _____

5. What part of the design is not ■ ? _____

6. What part of the design is not ■ ? _____

Create your own design in the grid using five different colors. Then write a fraction and a decimal for each colored part.

| Color | Fraction | Decimal |
|---|---|---|

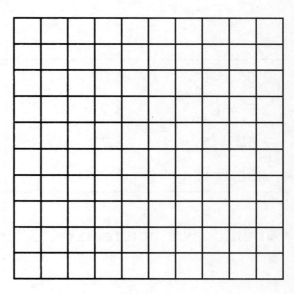

7. _____ _____ _____

8. _____ _____ _____

9. _____ _____ _____

10. _____ _____ _____

11. _____ _____ _____

**STRETCH YOUR THINKING   E131**

# Puzzling Decimals

Write the decimal for each number. Find the code letter
for each answer in the code box below. Write the code
letter under each answer. Your answers will solve a riddle.

1. five and two
   hundredths

2. $2\frac{56}{100}$

3. seven and
   three
   hundredths

4. three and
   seventy-seven
   hundredths

_____   _____   _____   _____

5. five and two
   tenths

6. $3\frac{7}{10}$

7. two and five
   hundredths

8. $2\frac{50}{100}$

_____   _____   _____   _____

9. two and five
   tenths

10. seven and
    three tenths

11. $3\frac{72}{100}$

12. seven and
    five tenths

_____   _____   _____   _____

13. three and
    seven
    hundredths

14. five and
    four tenths

15. $7\frac{35}{100}$

16. $5\frac{22}{100}$

_____   _____   _____   _____

| | | | |
|---|---|---|---|
| 2.05 = I | 3.07 = D | 5.02 = W | 7.03 = E |
| 2.5 = L | 3.7 = T | 5.2 = I | 7.3 = I |
| 2.50 = S | 3.72 = O | 5.22 = N | 7.35 = W |
| 2.56 = H | 3.77 = N | 5.4 = O | 7.5 = N |

When does a lion relax? _____

_____

# Creating Decimal Numbers

1. Write all of the decimal numbers you can make by placing the digits 1, 2, and 3 in each of the boxes below. Draw a ring around the largest number you make. Underline the smallest number you make.

☐.☐☐    ☐.☐☐

☐.☐☐    ☐.☐☐

☐.☐☐    ☐.☐☐

2. Write all of the decimal numbers you can make by placing the digits 2, 4, and 6 in each of the boxes below. Draw a ring around the largest number you make. Underline the smallest number you make.

☐☐.☐    ☐☐.☐

☐☐.☐    ☐☐.☐

☐☐.☐    ☐☐.☐

For Exercises 3–10, arrange digits in the boxes to make number sentences that are true. Use the digits 1, 3, and 5 in each number sentence.

3.  $1.00 <$ ☐.☐☐ $< 1.50$     4.  $3.00 <$ ☐.☐☐ $< 3.40$

5.  $3.10 <$ ☐.☐☐ $< 3.50$     6.  $5.00 <$ ☐.☐☐ $< 5.20$

7.  $10.0 <$ ☐☐.☐ $< 14.0$     8.  $30.0 <$ ☐☐.☐ $< 35.0$

9.  $50.0 <$ ☐☐.☐ $< 53.0$     10.  $1.50 <$ ☐.☐☐ $< 1.60$

# Picture Your Answer

---

**Jerry's Special Pizza — 10 slices**

$\frac{2}{10}$ of the slices have
only pepperoni

$\frac{4}{10}$ have only mushrooms

$\frac{3}{10}$ have only peppers

$\frac{1}{10}$ have only onions

---

For Exercises 1–4, write each answer as a fraction and then as a decimal.

1. What part of the pizza has either mushrooms or onions?

   _____

2. What part of the pizza has no pepperoni?

   _____

3. What part of the pizza has neither peppers nor onions?

   _____

4. What part of the pizza has either pepperoni or peppers?

   _____

For Problems 5–8, you may want to use grid paper to solve.

Each third-grade class is making a quilt that has 100 squares.

5. Mrs. Ito's class is using 3 colors: red, blue, and yellow. Of the 100 squares, 20 are red and 35 are yellow. Write a decimal to show what part of the squares are blue.

   _____

6. Mr. Quint's class is arranging 100 squares in a repeating pattern of red, white, and blue. Write a decimal to show what part of the squares are red.

   _____

7. Mr. Wakeham's class sewed a button on $\frac{1}{4}$ of the squares. Write a decimal to show what part of the squares have a button.

   _____

8. Mrs. Hart's class sewed hearts on 16 squares. Write a decimal to show what part of the squares do not have hearts.

   _____

# Choose the Best Unit

1. What is the best unit for measuring each item on the quilt? Use the key to color each triangle on the quilt.

| Key | |
|---|---|
| inch | red |
| foot or yard | yellow |
| mile | green |

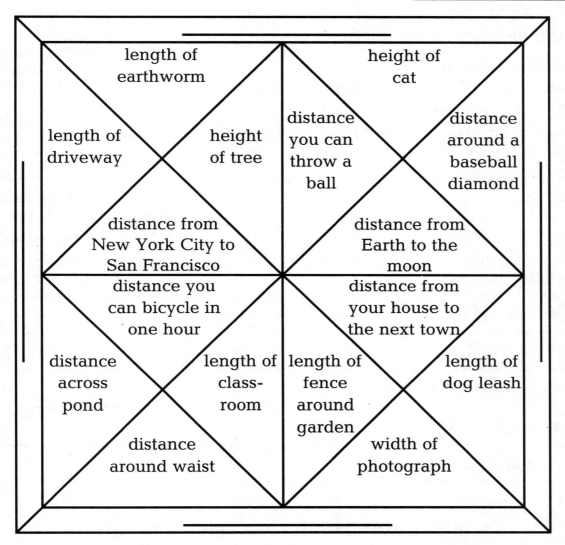

length of earthworm

height of cat

length of driveway

height of tree

distance you can throw a ball

distance around a baseball diamond

distance from New York City to San Francisco

distance from Earth to the moon

distance you can bicycle in one hour

distance from your house to the next town

distance across pond

length of class-room

length of fence around garden

length of dog leash

distance around waist

width of photograph

2. In the top border of the quilt, write an item to be measured in feet or yards. Color the top border yellow.

3. In the bottom border of the quilt, write an item to be measured in miles. Color the bottom border green.

4. In each side border of the quilt, write an item to be measured in inches. Color the side borders red.

# Body Measurements

You will need a ruler, yardstick, and string.

Look at your foot and estimate its length in inches. Record your estimate in the table. Then use a ruler to find the actual measurement to the nearest inch. Record the measure in the table.

Complete the table by recording your estimates and measurements. For Exercises 4–6, use a string to measure. Wrap the string around the body part and mark the string. Then measure that length of string by stretching it out on a ruler or yardstick.

| | Part of Your Body | Estimate | Measurement (to the nearest inch) |
|---|---|---|---|
| 1. | Length of foot | | |
| 2. | Length of hand (from wrist to longest fingertip) | | |
| 3. | Length of arm (from shoulder to longest fingertip) | | |
| 4. | Distance around head (where a cap would rest) | | |
| 5. | Distance around wrist | | |
| 6. | Distance around ankle | | |

7. Compare your estimates with the actual measurements. For which body part was your estimate the closest?

_____

8. Which is longer, the distance around your ankle or the length of your hand?

_____

# Logical Measuring

Measure and cut a 5-inch strip and a 2-inch strip from a piece of paper.

| 5 inches |
|---|

| 2 inches |
|---|

Use the two strips to measure the drawings in Exercises 1–4 to the nearest half inch. Do **not** use a ruler.

Hints:

- If you fold each strip in half, you will have two more measuring strips. Half of the 5-inch strip will be $2\frac{1}{2}$ inches long. Half of the 2-inch strip will be 1 inch long.

- You can compare or combine the rulers to form different lengths.

1. _____

2. _____

3. _____

4.

_____

5. Tell how you measured the pen in Exercise 1.

_____

_____

_____

# Reading a Map

Every inch on the map below stands for 1 mile of actual distance. Use your ruler on the map to learn the actual distance between places.

```
1 inch = 1 mile
```

Park

Library          School

1. Tom and Liz both live on the road between the library and the school. Tom lives 2 miles away from the library. Liz lives 1 mile away from the school. Draw and label dots on the map to show where Tom and Liz live.

2. How many miles is it from Tom's house to school? _____

3. How many miles is it from Liz's house to the library? _____

4. How many miles is it from Tom's house to Liz's house? _____

5. Sam lives on the same road as the park. He has to ride his bicycle 5 miles to get to Tom's house. Draw and label a dot on the map to show where Sam lives.

6. Liz rode her bicycle to the park and back home.

   How far did she ride? _____

7. Tom's father drove from his house to school and then

   to the library. How many miles did he drive? _____

# Making Sense of Measurements

Each box below makes a statement about capacity. Circle
the letters only in the boxes with sensible statements.
Form the answer to the riddle by writing the circled
letters in order on the blanks.

| | | |
|---|---|---|
| 1.     **A**<br>A punch bowl holds 10 gallons. | 2.     **Z**<br>A medicine bottle holds less than 1 cup. | 3.     **O**<br>A bathtub holds less than 3 quarts. |
| 4.     **E**<br>A tea kettle holds about 1 quart. | 5.     **R**<br>Beth drinks about 3 cups of milk a day. | 6.     **T**<br>An eyedropper holds about 1 cup. |
| 7.     **O**<br>Sam bought 2 quarts of ice cream for his party. | 8.     **S**<br>John's mug holds about 1 quart. | 9.     **C**<br>Mary and Liz shared a pint of juice. |
| 10.     **R**<br>The sink holds 20 gallons of water. | 11.     **U**<br>Mrs. Frank made 2 quarts of soup. | 12.     **E**<br>A car's gas tank holds less than 1 gallon. |
| 13.     **P**<br>Jane used 3 quarts of water to wash her lunch dishes. | 14.     **S**<br>Mr. Green made punch with 2 quarts of juice and 1 pint of sherbet. | 15.     **T**<br>Steve used 1 quart of milk in a cake recipe. |

How many cups of water can a funnel hold?

____ ____ ____ ____ ____    ____ ____ ____ ____

# Balancing Toys

Use the pictures to complete the sentences in Exercises 1–6.
Then use those sentences to answer Exercises 7–10.

**1.**

The whistle weighs _____ than the block.

**2.**

The car weighs _____ than the block.

**3.**

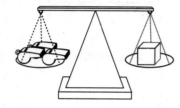

_____ whistles weigh the same as 1 block.

**4.**

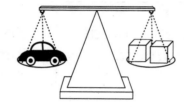

1 car weighs the same as _____ blocks.

**5.**

_____ balls weigh the same as 2 blocks.

**6.**

1 pencil weighs _____ than the block.

**7.** How many whistles weigh the same as 1 car?

_____

**8.** How many balls weigh the same as 1 car?

_____

A block weighs 3 ounces. Write the weight of the other toys.

**9.**

_____

**10.**

_____

**11.**

_____

# Metric Distances

The diagram shows the distance between some places in Oakville. Use the diagram to answer the questions.

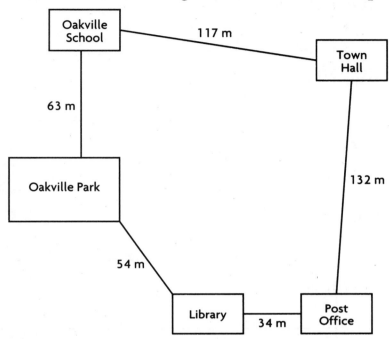

1. Tina left school and went to the town hall. Then she

   walked to the post office. How far did she go? _____

2. Larry walked from the town hall to Oakville School.
   Ron walked from Oakville School to the park. Who

   walked farther? How much farther? _____

3. Lisa walked from the library to the park and then to

   Oakville School. How far did she walk? _____

4. Mrs. Ruiz walked from the town hall to Oakville School

   and back. How far did she walk? _____

5. A letter carrier left the post office and delivered mail to
   the library. She walked back to the post office and picked
   up another delivery for the town hall. After making the
   delivery at the town hall, she returned to the post office.

   How far did she walk in all? _____

# What's the Order?

Order the lengths from shortest to longest.

1. 305 cm, 3 m, 31 dm, 360 cm, 35 dm

_____

2. 29 dm, 295 cm, 2 m, 2 dm, 29 m

_____

3. 155 cm, 15 m, 15 dm, 51 cm, 51 m

_____

4. 8m, 878 cm, 78 m, 87 dm, 787 cm

_____

5. 55 dm, 355 cm, 5 m, 535 cm, 35 m

_____

6. 986 cm, 86 m, 89 dm, 9 m, 96 dm

_____

7. 29 m, 92 dm, 290 cm, 909 cm, 229 dm

_____

8. Think of two places where you could apply what you learned about metric units of length.

_____

_____

9. Write a problem using data from one of the problems above. Solve.

_____

_____

_____

# Line Patterns

Use your ruler to find the pattern. Draw the next two lines.
Write the rule.

**1.** —————————
————————
—————————————

Rule:

_____

_____

**2.** ——————————————
————————
——————————

Rule:

_____

_____

**3.** ——
——————
————————————

Rule:

_____

_____

**4.** ——————
————————
————
——————————

Rule:

_____

_____

**5.** ————————————————
————————————
————————————

Rule:

_____

_____

**6.** ——————————
——————————
—————————

Rule:

_____

_____

# Combining Parts

Circle the two parts on the right that form the figure on
the left.

**1.**

**2.**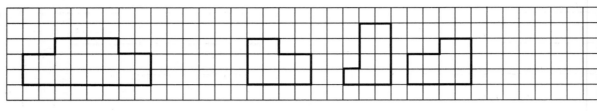

**3.**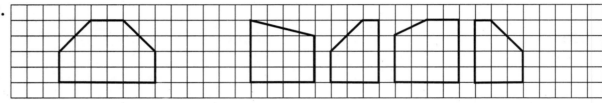

**4.**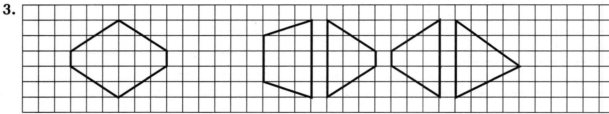

**5.**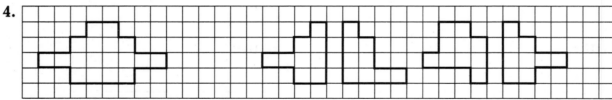

**6.**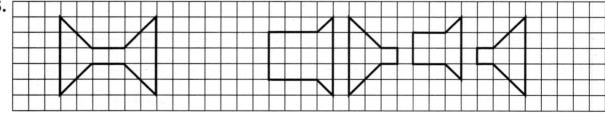

# Estimating and Comparing Capacity

Arrange the measurements from least to greatest capacity.

1. 5 L; 5,100 mL; 1,005 mL; 15 L; 1 L

_____

2. 2,950 mL; 3,120 mL; 3 L; 21 L; 2,130 mL

_____

3. 47 L; 7,040 mL; 4,770 mL; 4 L; 7,400 mL

_____

4. 6,500 mL; 5 L; 5,600 mL; 6 L; 5,066 mL

_____

5. 1,717 mL; 17 L; 107 mL; 71 L; 7,171 mL

_____

6. Think of objects that hold a liquid. Decide which
metric unit to use when measuring its capacity.
Complete the table.

| Object | Milliliters (mL) or Liters (L) |
|---|---|
| Bottle of maple syrup | mL |
| Bottle of water | L |
| | |
| | |

7. Write a problem using data from one of the
problems above. Solve.

_____

_____

# Graphing Mass

The masses of five students are shown in the table.

| Student | Mass |
|---------|------|
| Alice | 31 kg |
| Bob | 38 kg |
| Donna | 29 kg |
| Elia | 35 kg |
| Juan | 33 kg |

1. Use the table to create a bar graph.

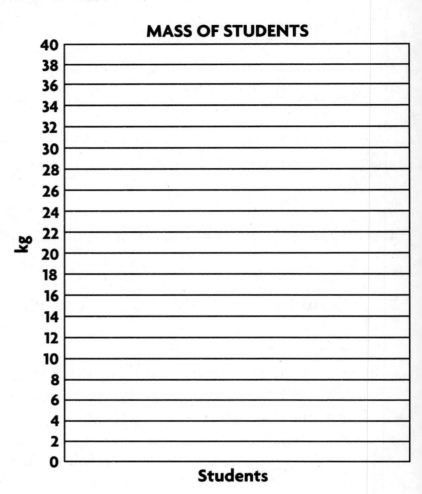

**MASS OF STUDENTS**

Students

2. What is the difference between the least and

   greatest mass shown in the graph? _____

3. What is the combined mass of Alice and Elia? _____

4. Order the students from least to greatest mass.

   _____

# Estimating and Measuring Perimeter

Estimate the perimeter of each figure in centimeters (cm).
Then use unit cubes or a centimeter ruler to find the actual
perimeter.

├─────┤
1 cm

**1.**

estimate: _____ cm

perimeter: _____ cm

**2.**

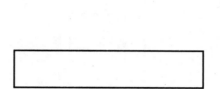

estimate: _____ cm

perimeter: _____ cm

**3.**

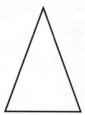

estimate: _____ cm

perimeter: _____ cm

**4.**

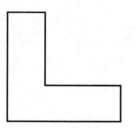

estimate: _____ cm

perimeter: _____ cm

**5.**

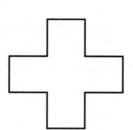

estimate: _____ cm

perimeter: _____ cm

**6.**

estimate: _____ cm

perimeter: _____ cm

**7.**

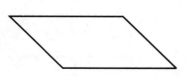

estimate: _____ cm

perimeter: _____ cm

**8.**

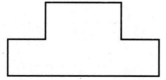

estimate: _____ cm

perimeter: _____ cm

**9.**

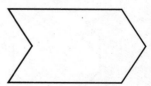

estimate: _____ cm

perimeter: _____ cm

Name _____

# Find the Missing Length

In each figure, a letter represents the length of one or more sides. Find the value of each letter by using the information that is given.

**1.**

perimeter = 8 units

a = _____ units

**2.**

perimeter = 16 units

b = _____ units

**3.**

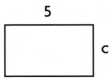

perimeter = 16 units

c = _____ units

**4.**

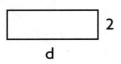

perimeter = 16 units

d = _____ units

**5.**

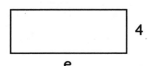

perimeter = 24 units

e = _____ units

**6.**

perimeter = 15 units

f = _____ units

**7.**

perimeter = 24 units

g = _____ units

**8.**

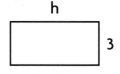

perimeter = 14 units

h = _____ units

**9.**

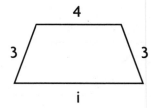

perimeter = 16 units

i = _____ units

# Areas in the Town

Find the area of each building in the town drawn on the grid below. Record your findings in the table.

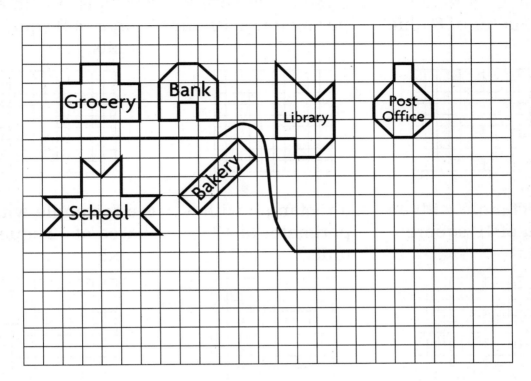

| | Building | Area |
|---|---|---|
| 1. | Grocery | ____ sq units |
| 2. | Bank | ____ sq units |
| 3. | School | ____ sq units |
| 4. | Library | ____ sq units |
| 5. | Post Office | ____ sq units |
| 6. | Bakery | ____ sq units |

7. Add a toy shop to the town. Make it have an area of 9 square units.

8. Add a restaurant to the town. Make it have the same area as the toy shop but a different shape.

# Drawing Shapes

Draw each shape as described.

**1.** a square with a
perimeter of 8 units

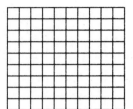

**2.** a rectangle with a
perimeter of 10 units

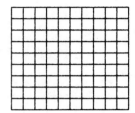

**3.** a square with an
area of 9 square
units

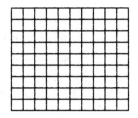

**4.** a rectangle with an
area of 10 square
units

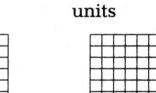

**5.** a rectangle with a
perimeter of 12
units

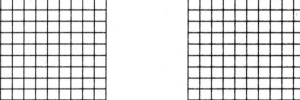

**6.** a rectangle with an
area of 12 square
units

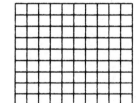

**7.** Draw a square and 2 rectangles that each have an
area of 16 square units.

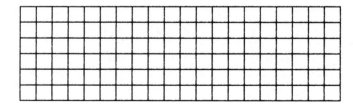

**8.** Draw 3 different shapes that each have a perimeter
of 14 units.

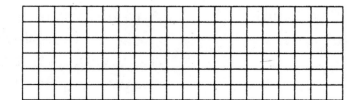

# Painting the Playroom

Amanda and her father are painting the walls of a playroom. One of the walls has a window. Another wall has a door, which they are not painting.

Find the area that needs to be painted on each of the four walls. All measurements are given in feet.

**1.**

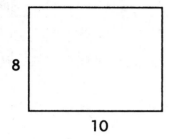

area = _____ sq ft

**2.**

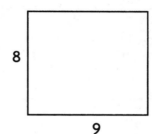

area = _____ sq ft

**3.**

area = _____ sq ft

**4.**

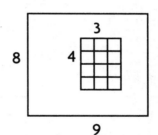

area = _____ sq ft

5. What is the total area that needs to be painted?

_____

6. The label on the can of paint says that 1 quart covers about 100 square feet. How many quarts of paint will Amanda and her father need to paint the walls with 2 coats of paint?

_____

7. Amanda wants to put a wallpaper border around the room near the ceiling. How many feet of wallpaper border does she need to go all the way around the room?

_____

# Sam's Supermarket

Sam displays his grocery items in rows. Look at the
pictures of the items Sam has in his supermarket.

- Use an array to find the total number of items in each display.
- Show how you found the product.

1.

_____

_____

2.

_____

3.

_____

_____

4.

_____

5.
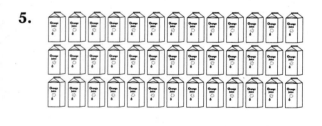

_____

6.

_____

7.

_____

_____

8.

_____

_____

# How Time Flies

Martin and Meg keep track of how long it takes them
to do certain activities. They also keep track of how
many times a week they do these activities.

Martin and Meg each record their results in a table.

| MARTIN | | |
|---|---|---|
| Activity | Time It Takes | Number of Times per Week |
| Brush Teeth | 2 min | 14 |
| Eat Breakfast | 12 min | 7 |
| Take Shower | 15 min | 7 |
| Walk to School | 10 min | 5 |

| MEG | | |
|---|---|---|
| Activity | Time It Takes | Number of Times per Week |
| Brush Teeth | 1 min | 21 |
| Eat Breakfast | 10 min | 7 |
| Take Shower | 18 min | 7 |
| Walk to School | 12 min | 5 |

**Make a model to solve.**

1. How many minutes per week does Martin spend eating breakfast?

   _____

2. How many minutes per week does Meg spend walking to school?

   _____

3. Does Martin spend more time brushing his teeth each week or walking to school?

   _____

4. Does Meg spend more time eating her breakfast each week or walking to school?

   _____

5. Who spends more time each week brushing teeth?

   _____

6. Who spends more than 2 hours a week taking showers?

   _____

7. a. How long does it take you to brush your teeth? _____

   b. How many times a week do you brush your teeth? _____

   c. How much time each week do you spend brushing

      your teeth? _____

# Figure Fun

$\square = 100$     $\triangle = 10$     $\bigcirc = 1$

Replace each shape with its value. Find the product.
Then write the answer by using symbols.

**Example**   △△○○
               × ○○○

$10 + 10 + 1 + 1 = 22$     $\begin{array}{r} 22 \\ \times\ 3 \\ \hline 66 \end{array}$     $66 = $ △△△○○○
                                                                                      △△△○○○

$1 + 1 + 1 = 3$

---

1.   △△○○○○
     × ___ ○○○

_____

2.   △△△○○
     × ___ ○○

_____

3.   △△△△○
     × ___ ○○○○

_____

4.   △△△○○○○○
     × ___ ○○○○○○

_____

5.   △△○○○○○○○
     × ___ ○○○

_____

6.   △△△△○
     × ○○○○○○○

_____

7.   △△△△△○○○○○
     × ___ ○○○○○

_____

8.   △△○○○○○○○○○○
     × ___ ○○○○○○

_____

9.   △○○○○○○○
     × ○○○○○○○

_____

10.   △△△△○○○○
      × ___ ○○○○

_____

11.   △△△○○○○○
      × ___ ○○○○

_____

12.   △○○○○○
      × ___ ○○○

_____

# Picture This!

Each picture below represents a number. Solve the problem.
Then match the picture letter to the product.

$\text{🌼}=0$ , $\heartsuit=1$ , $\square=2$ , $\bigcirc=3$ , $\triangle=4$ , $\text{🌳}=5$ , $\text{⛵}=6$ , $\text{☀}=7$ , $\text{📖}=8$ , $\diamondsuit=9$

## Example

$$\begin{array}{r} 27 \\ \times\ 4 \\ \hline 108 \end{array}$$

$108 = \heartsuit \ \text{🌼} \ \text{📖}$

**1.**  $\begin{array}{r} 65 \\ \times\ 4 \\ \hline \end{array}$  _____

**2.**  $\begin{array}{r} 36 \\ \times\ 6 \\ \hline \end{array}$  _____

**3.**  $\begin{array}{r} 47 \\ \times\ 4 \\ \hline \end{array}$  _____

**4.**  $\begin{array}{r} 52 \\ \times\ 2 \\ \hline \end{array}$  _____

**5.**  $\begin{array}{r} 32 \\ \times\ 5 \\ \hline \end{array}$  _____

**6.**  $\begin{array}{r} 48 \\ \times\ 3 \\ \hline \end{array}$  _____

**7.**  $\begin{array}{r} 21 \\ \times\ 6 \\ \hline \end{array}$  _____

**8.**  $\begin{array}{r} 28 \\ \times\ 3 \\ \hline \end{array}$  _____

| PICTURE NUMBERS | | |
|---|---|---|
| **A** | $\heartsuit$ | 🌼 $\triangle$ |
| **B** | $\heartsuit$ | 📖 📖 |
| **C** | $\heartsuit$ | ⛵ 🌼 |
| **D** | $\square$ | $\heartsuit$ ⛵ |
| **E** | $\heartsuit$ | $\triangle$ $\triangle$ |
| **F** | $\heartsuit$ | $\square$ ⛵ |
| **G** | $\square$ | ⛵ 🌼 |
| **H** | 📖 | $\triangle$ |

# Can You Find Me?

Solve the problems below. Then find the answers in the
number search. Circle the answers. You will find them
upward, downward, diagonal, and backward.

| 2 | 2 | 0 | 1 | 4 | 0 | 7 | 7 | 1 | 1 | 0 |
|---|---|---|---|---|---|---|---|---|---|---|
| 5 | 9 | 1 | 3 | 4 | 6 | 2 | 3 | 7 | 2 | 9 |
| 7 | 4 | 0 | 0 | 2 | 5 | 8 | 3 | 0 | 3 | 8 |
| 4 | 3 | 9 | 2 | 5 | 0 | 4 | 1 | 3 | 0 | 6 |
| 6 | 5 | 1 | 4 | 1 | 5 | 5 | 4 | 1 | 8 | 8 |
| 2 | 1 | 6 | 3 | 6 | 0 | 1 | 7 | 4 | 1 | 5 |
| 1 | 0 | 0 | 1 | 4 | 2 | 6 | 9 | 5 | 8 | 0 |
| 4 | 7 | 4 | 5 | 0 | 4 | 2 | 0 | 1 | 1 | 4 |
| 1 | 8 | 5 | 3 | 3 | 6 | 8 | 5 | 6 | 2 | 3 |
| 2 | 0 | 1 | 5 | 1 | 6 | 0 | 8 | 0 | 0 | 1 |

1. $56 \times 6 =$ _____

2. $41 \times 3 =$ _____

3. $24 \times 3 =$ _____

4. $58 \times 5 =$ _____

5. $98 \times 3 =$ _____

6. $12 \times 8 =$ _____

7. $54 \times 4 =$ _____

8. $67 \times 2 =$ _____

9. $10 \times 7 =$ _____

10. $26 \times 6 =$ _____

11. $23 \times 8 =$ _____

12. $94 \times 2 =$ _____

13. $71 \times 2 =$ _____

14. $39 \times 2 =$ _____

15. $64 \times 5 =$ _____

16. $14 \times 4 =$ _____

17. $29 \times 9 =$ _____

18. $31 \times 5 =$ _____

# Sharing Marbles

Meg, Tony, and Rich want to share 26 marbles evenly.
They decide to put any extra marbles in a jar.

1. How many marbles will each friend get? _____

2. How many marbles will they put in the jar? _____

Finish this table to show other ways of sharing.

| | Number of Marbles | Number of Friends | Marbles for Each Friend | Leftover Marbles |
|---|---|---|---|---|
| 3. | 34 | 4 | | |
| 4. | 29 | 6 | | |
| 5. | 26 | 3 | | |
| 6. | 33 | | 5 | |
| 7. | 15 | | 7 | |
| 8. | 23 | | 3 | |
| 9. | | 4 | 3 | 2 |
| 10. | | 3 | 7 | 1 |
| 11. | | 6 | 5 | 4 |

12. A group of 5 friends wants to share a set of stickers evenly. What is the greatest number of stickers that could be left over?

_____

13. A group of friends shares a batch of cookies evenly. There are 3 cookies left over. What is the least number of friends that could be in the group?

_____

# Number Sentences

Complete the number sentences that describe each picture.

---

**1.** $3 \times 24 =$ _____

**2.** $72 \div 3 =$ _____

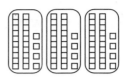

---

**3.** $4 \times$ _____ $= 56$

**4.** $56 \div$ _____ $= 14$

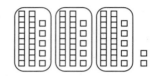

---

**5.** $3 \times 25 = 75$; $75 + 2 =$ _____

**6.** $77 \div 3 = 25$ r _____

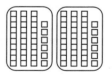

---

Write one number sentence using multiplication and one
number sentence using division to describe each picture.
If there is a remainder, you will also need to write a
number sentence using addition.

---

**7.** _____

**8.** _____

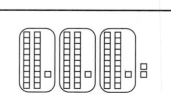

---

**9.** _____

**10.** _____

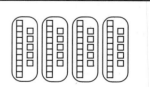

---

**11.** _____

**12.** _____

---

# Arranging Digits

Max has made up 6 different division problems using only
the digits 2, 4, and 6. He is wondering which problems will
have the largest and smallest quotients. Find the quotient
for each problem.

1. 2)  4  6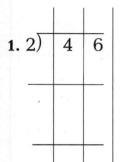

2. 2)  6  4

3. 4)  2  6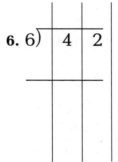

4. 4)  6  2

5. 6)  2  4

6. 6)  4  2

7. Circle the largest quotient.

8. Draw a star next to the smallest quotient.

Make up your own division problems by arranging the
digits 3, 5, and 7 in different ways. Solve each problem.

9.

10.

11.

12.

13.

14.

# The Division Race

Choose a partner.

**Materials**: Number cube, game token for each player, scratch paper and pencil

**How to Play**: Place game tokens on Start. Take turns rolling the number cube. Use the number rolled as the divisor for the number on your space. Use scratch paper to divide. Then, move the number of spaces shown in the remainder. If there is no remainder, do not move. The first player to cross the finish line is the winner.

**Example**: Player's marker is on 86. Player rolls 3.
$86 \div 3 = 28$ r2. Move 2 spaces.

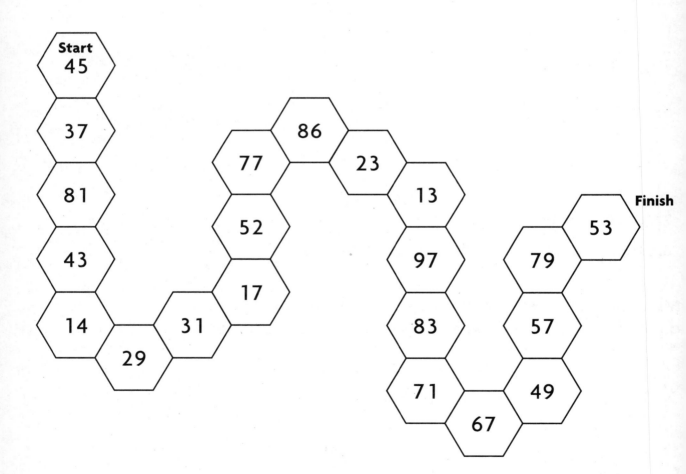

# Planning a Picnic

Mrs. Ellis is planning a
picnic for 48 people.
Use the chart to help
her plan the picnic.

| Hot dogs | 8 in a package |
|---|---|
| Hot dog buns | 6 in a package |
| Juice | 64 ounces in a bottle |
| Chips | 9 servings in a bag |
| Apples | 10 in a bag |

1. How many packages of hot
   dogs would give each person
   2 hot dogs?

   _____

2. How many packages of hot
   dog buns would give each
   person 2 hot dog buns?

   _____

3. One bottle of juice will give
   how many people an 8-ounce
   serving?

   _____

4. How many bags of apples
   would give each person one
   apple? How many extra
   apples would there be?

   _____

5. How many bags of chips
   would give each person one
   serving? How many extra
   servings would there be?

   _____

6. How many cookies should
   Mrs. Ellis bake so that each
   person can have
   2 cookies?

   _____

7. Each picnic table can seat
   8 people. The 30 children
   all want to sit together.
   How many tables will
   they need?

   _____

8. Mrs. Ellis buys a package of
   250 napkins. If each person
   uses 2 napkins, how many
   napkins will be left after
   the picnic?

   _____

# Using the Clues

Write a number sentence to solve. Use the underlined
words to help you find the solution.

1. Mrs. Scott washed 52 socks.
How many <u>pairs</u> of socks did
she wash?

_____

_____

2. Dan has $92 in the bank. Joe
has <u>triple</u> that amount. How
much money does Joe have?

_____

_____

3. Mr. French told his
27 students to form groups.
How many <u>threesomes</u>
could they form?

_____

_____

4. Pam is reading a book that is
225 pages long. She has read
a <u>third</u> of the book. How many
pages has she read?

_____

_____

5. There are 42 singers in the
chorus. How many <u>trios</u> could
be formed?

_____

_____

6. There are 38 <u>couples</u> dancing
at the dance. How many peo-
ple are dancing?

_____

_____

7. The Brown family drove
158 miles on Saturday. On
Sunday, they drove <u>twice</u> as
far. How many miles did they
drive on Sunday?

_____

_____

8. On Monday, 96 people
attended the book fair. On
Tuesday, only <u>half</u> as many
people attended. How many
people attended the book fair
on Tuesday?

_____

_____